VOID
Library of
Davidson College

Sylvie Debevec Henning

GENET'S RITUAL PLAY

GENET'S RITUAL PLAY

GENET'S RITUAL PLAY

by

Sylvie Debevec Henning

AMSTERDAM 1981

DEGRÉ SECOND 6

© Editions Rodopi BV., Amsterdam 1981
Printed in the Netherlands
ISBN: 90-6203-773-9

Sur une scène presque semblable aux nôtre, sur une estrade, il s'agissait de reconstituer la fin d'un repas. A partir de cette seule donnée qu'on y retrouve à peine, le plus haut drame moderne s'est exprimé pendant deux mille ans et tous les jours dans le sacrifice de la messe. Le point de départ disparaît sous la profusion des ornements et des symboles qui nous bouleversent encore. Sous les apparences les plus familières--une croûte de pain--on y dévore un dieu. Théâtralement, je ne sais rien de plus efficace que l'élévation.

"Lettre à Pauvert," <u>L'Atelier</u>
<u>d'Alberto Giacometti</u>--<u>Les Bonnes</u>

CONTENTS

I	INTRODUCTION	3
II.1	SACRIFICIAL MIMESIS	7
II.2	IM-PLICATIONS	37
III	SACRAMENTAL ELEVATION	84
IV	CREATIVE POSSIBILITIES	105

I   INTRODUCTION

Most discussions of the ritualistic dimension of Genet's theater focus on merely superficial similarities either with the Catholic Mass or with its inversion, the Black Mass. Genet, in his "Lettre à Pauvert," makes the former relation explicit. Critics have seized upon this passage without considering carefully enough its internal complexities, the nature of its reference to the sacrificial elevation, or the Catholic rite itself. Perhaps the first commentator to describe <u>Les Bonnes</u> as a satanic Mass, on the other hand, was Jean-Paul Sartre. The idea was subsequently developed by R. A. Zimbardo in "Genet's Black Mass."[1] Neither view, however, does justice to the actual articulation of Genet's theater. First, each usually overlooks the tensely dual nature of the Mass itself, i.e., the fact that it includes many primitive, as well as more strictly Christian, elements. Each then consequently remains unable to offer an interpretation adequate to the truly intricate, and perhaps contestatory (even self-contestatory), conception of ritual that informs Genet's writing. In <u>Les Bonnes</u>

that conception becomes especially apparent. Here Genet seeks to incorporate (as the Mass itself in fact does) both the cyclical and immanent, on the one hand, and the teleological and transcendent on the other. In doing so, however, he manages to maintain (as the Mass, according at least to the "orthodox" interpretation, does not) an important degree of active, vital interinvolvement between the two religious perspectives.

This essay will first attempt to demonstrate, then, that <u>Les Bonnes</u>, while seeming to repeat the pattern of the primitive periodic rites, actually modifies that pattern in significant ways. This significance, moreover, consists especially in the way the specific modifications appear to interrogate the established idea of cyclical regeneration. Similarly, this essay will also consider how the play, while apparently seeking the ritualistically achieved totalization or oneness that would seem the expressed <u>telos</u> of the Christian liturgy, raises doubts about that very possibility. Thus, Genet may be seen both to employ traditional cultural forms and, through his particular modes of employment, simultaneously to question or challenge our usual understanding of them. It may then also be the case, however, that the "violence" thereby done to both ritual patterns does not at all lead, as earlier critics have suggested, only to the sterile impasse of either hollow repetition or thwarted attempts at sublated reconciliation. Rather, it may in fact reveal certain ambiguities within and between what are normally considered clear and distinct categories or relations. These specific instances of cultural "violence" may uncover, in other words, the "play" within the familiar ritual structures and the interplay between them. Meaningful "play" of this sort has recently been interpreted by René Girard as a symptom of the "sacrificial crisis" that threatens to destroy the existing social order.[2] Sartre purports to see in it a more solipsistic function, viz., that of a mere personal escape by poetic means from an ontological gallery of mirrors. This essay will argue that such play within and between categories or structures (rather like Derrida's "regulated play" or Heidegger's Spielraum) may, on the contrary, be a constructive, dynamic force, in some ways unhinging (and therefore, in a sense, threatening) an existing structure, but in order also to make room for the further development of its resources, for the exploration of its still inherent possibilities, or for yet more radical transformations and discoveries. In this way, playful ambiguity, because it announces the potentially regenerative questioning of established forms and categories, a questioning fundamental to the exhilaration of all inventive art, may in itself open up truly creative opportunities within the very tradition it unsettles.

NOTES

[1] Jean-Paul Sartre, <u>Saint Genet: Comédien et martyr</u> (Paris: Gallimard, 1952), p. 569; R. A. Zimbardo, "Genet's Black Mass," <u>Modern Drama</u>, no. 8 (December, 1965), pp. 247-58.

[2] René Girard, <u>Violence and the Sacred</u>, trans. R. Gregory (1977; rpt. Baltimore: Johns Hopkins University Press, 1979).

II.1 SACRIFICIAL MIMESIS

Turning to Genet's peculiar relation to primitive pagan celebrations, we find that it has, in the first place, largely been ignored by critics, although many of the textual elements brought together below have previously been treated in isolation. A close reading of Les Bonnes reveals, however, that the maids preserve something like the form of these archaic rites in the ritualistic ceremony they repeatedly enact. This essay aims, therefore, first to demonstrate that what have generally been treated as individual themes--e.g., role playing, reversal, and exchange--can be mutually related, and then, beyond this, taken together and related structurally to a larger, and historically significant, world-view: a specifically cyclical one, based on repetition and periodic return to an origin. Nevertheless, the maids' personal ritual is not simply a copy of any "archetype." The archaic model has been modified by the play so as to heighten and bring out certain problematic elements already present in the "original" rite itself, albeit latent, and therefore usually unacknowledged.

We may begin, then, by noting that in many primitive societies the great yearly festivals are those of return and renewal. In a broad sense it may be said that such ceremonies have as their function the casting out of whatever elements have become deadly to the community and the bringing (back) in of whatever gives it life. Frazer and the Cambridge Ritualists emphasized the seasonal and agricultural connotations of the festive cycles. Durkheim, however, insisted that the seasons only furnished an outer framework for the rituals whose real function was to revitalize and reinforce the sense of <u>communitas</u> or the perfect communal identity among equals. More recently, Girard has centered his interpretation on society's recurring need to purge itself of violence through the death of a sacrificial victim.[1]

These ritual scenarios, however, may take many specific forms. The one at issue here has been closely associated with the historically familiar forms of carnival life: the enthronement, dethronement and "execution" of a mock monarch who serves as a communal scapegoat. It has been argued, moreover, that this carnival anti-king is in fact only a ritual substitute for an original <u>pharmakos</u>, either real king or initial surrogate, actually executed when the sovereign's powers had degenerated. His elimination puts an end to the disorder provoked by the community's failures, cleanses it, and allows it to be born anew in full vigor and health.[2] In such rites, dethronement and death are, it appears, effective complements of enthronement and cannot be separated from it.

In turning to <u>Les Bonnes</u> itself we find it does indeed repeat the pattern of this archaic rite. As the play opens we witness the enthronement of a ceremonial Madame, for what we see is merely the maids' glorified portrayal of their employer. It is not, however, until the alarm clock rings that the spectators realize this "Madame" is only a substitute. Sarcastic, insulting, she is a caricature of the <u>patronne</u>. Like the ceremonial sovereign of tradition, she is designed to represent what Girard has described as "a monster of iniquity," "the paragon of transgressors . . . who holds nothing sacred and who fearlessly assumes every form of <u>hubris</u>."[3] She refuses all contact with whatever might defile her, whether the rubber gloves that wash her china, the spittle that polishes her shoes, or the odor and breath of her maid. "Tenez vos mains loin des miennes, votre contact est immonde."[4] This living icon must be kept at a distance from all that is profane, a sacred statue surrounded by flowers on its processional altar: ". . . vous m'élevez un reposoir" (p. 54). "Regarde ces corolles ouvertes en mon honneur! Je suis une Vierge plus belle, Claire," says "Madame" to her kneeling servant (p. 20).[5] This degree of distance (as well as the absence of the maids' real employer) is further emphasized by the use of third person address. Traditionally it served to set apart and exalt the dominant class. Here, during the sisters' dramatized depiction of their relation to Madame, it also transforms the latter into a nonperson, an absent object.[6] Or rather, it heightens the ambiguity of the scene. Madame is, in a sense (and one to which we shall return below), simultaneously present and absent. In addition, her possessions, the concrete manifestations of her status--dresses, jewels, furs, cosmetics--become, during the ceremony, ritual accessories to be handled with the same reverence as Madame herself.

> Jamais nous ne pourrons rempla-
> cer Madame. Si Madame connais-
> sait nos précautions pour arran-
> ger ses toilettes! L'armoire de
> Madame, c'est pour nous comme la
> chapelle de la Sainte-Vierge.
> Quand nous l'ouvrons . . . Nous
> l'ouvrons à deux battants, nos
> jours de fête. Nous pouvons à
> peine regarder les robes, nous
> n'avons pas le droit. L'armoire
> de Madame est sacrée. C'est sa
> grande penderie! (p. 63).

After her exaltation, however, this false Madame, like the ceremonial king, is debased and her sacred objects defiled. Hands once kept at a distance now strike and buffet; words of admiration become insults; vestments are soiled.

> Je vous hais! Je hais votre
> poitrine pleine de souffles em-
> baumés. Votre . . . poitrine
> . . . d'ivoire. Vos cuisses . . .
> d'or! Vos pieds . . . d'ambre!
> (Elle crache sur la robe rouge.)
> (p. 24)

This passage is all the more blasphemous because of the sexual connotations it lends to certain elements of the litany of the Virgin Mary (Tower of Ivory, House of Gold). Even the <u>glaïeuls</u> with which the maids adoringly decorate Madame's bedroom call forth the <u>glaviaux</u> that profanate, as in the narrator's imagined encounter with his mother in <u>Le Journal du voleur</u>.[7]

"Madame" is evidently about to be executed when an alarm clock rings, bringing this phase of the ritual to what, from the perspective of tradition, must constitute a premature end. Yet, it subsequently appears that the similacrum of ritual has intentionally been made too long for its traditional culmination ever in fact to be reached.

> Solange: C'est chaque fois pareil. Et par ta faute. Tu n'es jamais prête assez vite. Je ne peux pas t'achever.
> Claire: Ce qui nous prend du temps, c'est les préparatifs (p. 27).

Thus, the primitive ceremony is not really enacted in its murderous, historical form, but instead has already begun to undergo some modification.

Nevertheless, despite this mise à mort manquée, the maids' employer does indeed return to assume her place, so that the traditional cycle is apparently completed after all. This too, however, turns out to be merely an image. The true patronne, we now learn, is no more than a paramour of the absent Monsieur, a kept-woman, and not really the mistress of a genuine bourgeois household. Opposite the feigned obedience and kindness of her "Loyal Servants," she plays the Faithful Woman, willing to follow the Man She Loves into Darkest Torments. Paradoxically, the maids' earlier impersonation, intended as a hateful caricature, now appears to have conferred upon Madame a dignity she does not in fact possess. Following Girard, one might well argue that the goal of this impersonation was to make the maids' victim wholly sacrificeable by exaggerating her traits. In this way, they would diminish the degree of similarity between themselves and their mistress to whom they are otherwise so closely related. Only such "sacrificial preparation" could put the proper distance between them.[8] In any case, it now seems that Claire played the archetypal mistress better than her employer; the latter is the real parody. As an obvious phony, Madame is particularly ridiculous because her actions must now appear derisory copies of the maids' more powerful ritual gestures. Madame herself is only one more substitute monarch, and the cycle begins again. The maids', however, do not now dare to defile their employer openly. In her actual presence they are compelled bitterly to recite the litany of her favors. "Je me récite les bontés de Madame (pp. 72-4). Any assaults upon her can be only surreptitiously attempted. It is consequently no surprise that they are destined to fail.

Having refused a cup of secretly poisoned tea, Madame departs, leaving the maids to continue the rite alone. Claire now still dressed in her little black uniform, again assumes the role of "Madame," while Solange, arrayed in white, becomes "Claire." There is no longer any need to enthrone the mock sovereign; the maids, by their reactions to their employer, have already done so. "Passez sur les formalités du début . . . Aux insultes" (p. 81). It appears, then, that the scene between the <u>patronne</u> and her maids has served here as the traditional exaltation segment of the ceremony. Thus, the "reality"/ritual distinction becomes, in effect, somewhat blurred. But it is never entirely erased, for after the sacred image of Madame is once again profanated, its destruction is still only simulated when the maid merely pretends to strangle her "mistress." Here, however, the ritual ceremony takes a new turn. At last, it seems, the substitute victim will truly be destroyed.

Now, in the primitive <u>fête</u>, between the ritual removal of the old king and the accession of the "reborn" one, normal life is in a state of suspension while the mock sovereign rules. Roger Caillois has called this festive period "le règne du sacré," a return to "le Grand Temps mythique" during which "l'extraordinaire [est] la règle." The everyday profane world is turned upside-down as rules are suspended, normal relationships reversed and, in general, license recommended. This topsy-turvy period is, in addition, fundamentally ambiguous. It is viewed simultaneously as a revival of the

Golden Age of egalitarian harmony and as a return to the chaos of barbarous emotions and monstrous excess.⁹ It is, in short, a period of what Girard would call seeming lack of sufficient differentiation.

Traditionally, the most fundamental of ritual reversals, once preserved in the Kalends and Saturnalia, is that in which men dress in female attire. "L'échange des vêtements," explains Caillois, "apparaît comme la signature même de l'état de chaos, comme le symbole du renversement des valeurs." Girard goes further in pointing out that such reversals signal a general loss of sexual differentiation. "[O]ne of the effects of the sacrificial crisis is a certain feminization of the men, accompanied by a masculinization of the women."¹⁰ Sartre has suggested that the female roles in Les Bonnes were supposed to be assumed by young men. He bases this assertion on the words of the narrator in Notre Dame des Fleurs: "S'il me fallait faire représenter une pièce théâtrale où des femmes auraient un rôle, j'exigerais que ce rôle fût tenu par des adolescents."¹¹ It will later be shown that, even if this, rather indirect, suggestion is not taken, Solange and Claire will nevertheless contest the very idea of "womanliness." Yet no true reciprocity is here possible even if the sisters were merely men in disguise, since there are no male roles to be played by women as ritual reversal requires. Monsieur and Mario, the male presence in the play, are effectively absent, never once appearing on stage.

The distinction between the free and the servile is also abolished or inverted during the archaic period of license. Masters and slaves exchange places, the latter now giving orders and laying down the law, the former awaiting their beck and call.[12] So too with the maids, though not without a significant difference. Claire does indeed assume the behavior of her mistress, but during the maids' private ceremony it is Solange, not Madame, who plays the servant's part. The ritual reversal of roles is thus only partially achieved, and the servants can only degrade themselves. When the false Madame affronts her servant, it is still, as ever, one of the maids who must suffer. The rite is already rigged so that the relationship maid/mistress cannot be truly inverted. Madame will never play her ritual role. No true reciprocity is possible in this sense either.

    The other side of the fête, a return to the chaos of violent emotions, is not, however, lacking. Claire and Solange hate one another, though it is hatred mixed with love. "Elles se haïssent d'amour," as Sartre explains.[13] The more obvious love-hatred of the sisters for Madame mingles at the same time with that which they feel for each other and which each also feels for herself. Since such reciprocal and indeed sororal violence (Solange and Claire being, then, "enemy sisters") is seen by Girard as the essence of the sacrificial crisis commemorated by ritual (and as in fact "identical" to the social and sexual non-differentiation noted earlier as the other major characteristic of the fête), it is important that we now attempt to evaluate the play from the point of view of what he calls "triangular anxiety" or "violent mimesis."

    Girard assumes the necessity of three elements in order to establish a relationship of violent mimesis: the subject, the object, and the rival. The dominant role is accorded to the latter. To assert this is to conclude, says Girard, that "rivalry does not arise because of the fortuitous convergence of <u>two desires on a single object</u>; rather <u>the subject desires the object because the rival desires it</u>." Such "mimesis coupled with desire leads automatically to conflict." The reciprocal relationship is completed when Girard adds that "the disciple can also serve as a model, even to his own model." Indeed, the model "invariably assumes the role of disciple . . . "[14]

In <u>Les Bonnes</u>, we find evidence of a complex network of what are, indeed, mimetic relationships. The first and most obvious has been ritualized in the maids' nightly ceremony: Solange and Claire "imitate" their relationship of subjugation to Madame. In this case, the object of desire is somewhat obscure, but ultimately it can only be Madame herself, for the maids (as portrayed by Solange) and "Madame" (as portrayed by Claire) desire (to be) Madame, the <u>patronne</u>. The sisters would like, that is, both to accede to the latter's status with all the power it would bring over others like themselves and, at least latently, even to possess her physically. This implies two rivalries of the sort Girard describes. First, <u>the maids stand together against their employer</u>. Both sides desire the status of bourgeois mistress: the one side to acquire it, the other to retain it. In addition, underlying, or superimposed upon, this relation to their employer (either is plausible), there would be a second Girardian rivalry, an "internal" one between the two sis- ters for possession of the desired object, whether status, Madame herself, or both. Simultaneously, of course, the sisters are rivals for the absent Mario. But, initially at least, this does not seem to constitute part of the ritual, belonging instead to "reality," and is therefore out of place at this point of the discussion. Later, we will see how problematic this frequently helpful distinction can in fact become. We should, however, call attention to the difficulty, if not the impossibility, of telling which of the characters desired the "object" first and who, then, is consequently imitating whom. Clearly, Madame is the initial possessor of the status involved, but that does not settle the question of desire, hence of mimetic desire. Between Claire and Solange, there is no way of knowing which, or whether, one sister craved that status first. Where physical possession is at issue, it is similarly clear that Madame herself is not even a rival in any significant sense, while between the sisters there is, once again, no way of telling whether one sister has been the initiator of such desire. Nevertheless, this obvious relation, or network of relations, of mimetic desire does seem to exist.

Given this basic mimetic relationship, one might subsequently want to ask why the maids project such a cruel and haughty image of the <u>patronne</u>, an image that turns their actual employer into a caricature of herself. The response might be that such a portrait, by exalting Madame in this fearsome way, justifies the sisters' adoration and thus makes worthwhile their apparently sought-after participation in her status. At the same time, her seemingly unjust treatment of them explains their revolt. More importantly, perhaps, Claire and Solange, by glorifying Madame, debase themselves, so that, through a caricaturization of the master/servant relationship, each can reveal her hatred of the other and, ipso facto, of herself. Sartre has in fact interpreted <u>Les Bonnes</u> in much this way.[15] Following Girard, we might arrive at another interpretation. The parody of Madame is an attempt to deny at least one essential aspect of the obvious rivalry. The model is projected far above the disciple, so that the latter may see himself as too unworthy even to entertain the notion that he and his model are rivals with identical desires.

The maids, however, also play at being maids. In the rite, "Claire" appears both more humble and more insolent than otherwise. Perhaps she appears more humble because this is how the archetypal maid should act in the presence of her mistress, and more insolent because this is how the archetypal servant should seem in her eyes or in revolt. Why such contradictory attributes? The portrait of the humiliated maid we have already posited as the corollary of the mimetic desire for Madame and her status. The defiant maid would then be the role the sisters actually desire for themselves qua maids. Both Claire and Solange as genuine maids, and Solange as the false Claire, desire (to be) such a maid. As with the imitation of Madame, they appear both to desire to accede to the status of bonne révoltée and, at least latently, to possess her physically. Consider, in this regard, the retrospective description of the maids' ritual provided by Genet in "Comment jouer Les Bonnes": ["Leur oeil est pur, très pur, puisque tous les soirs elles se masturbent et déchargent en vrac, l'une dans l'autre leur haine de Madame."[16] This dimension of the sexual desire implied in the play might then be both masturbatory, if the desired maid is identified with the one who desires, and homosexual and incestuous, if she is identified with the other sister.

A further relation of triangular desire should be mentioned here, even though it occurs "outside" the rite, because it parallels in the domain of the "profane" the relationships of the rite itself. We have already discovered that Madame as patronne is a fake. She is only an imitation, a merely possible version of the ideal: "un peu cocotte et un peu bourgeoise."[17] Thus, in "reality," too, the maids and their patronne are rivals, each aspiring to the position of true social authority. Neither side is disposed to acknowledge this rivalry however. Girard observes that "the model, even when he has openly encouraged imitation, is surprised to find himself engaged in competition. He concludes that the disciple has betrayed his confidence by following in his footsteps." Madame does freely give her servants old clothes and make-up, in effect overtly saying, "Imitate me!" She seems, however, more amused than indignant when they do.

> Ce n'est pas de la poudre, c'est du fard, c'est de la "cendre de roses", un vieux rouge dont je ne me sers plus. Tu as raison. Tu es encore jeune, embellis-toi, ma fille. Arrange-toi. (Elle lui met une fleur dans les cheveux. . . .) (p. 70).

"As for the disciple," Girard continues, "he feels both rejected and humiliated, judged unworthy by his model of participating in the superior existence the model himself enjoys."[18] Although Madame herself does not overtly scorn them, the sisters do seem to interpret her actions as signs of a condescension that in fact reinforces the social distance between them. Madame's generosity serves only to degrade them in their own eyes, reminding them of their inferior status: "Jamais nous ne pourrons remplacer Madame" (p. 63). As expected in Girard's theory, such an obvious "double bind," i.e., the contradictory encouragement of imitation and ridicule of that imitation, leads to violence against Madame, or at least to attempted violence, for neither strangulation nor poisoning actually succeeds. But why do these attempts fail? It appears that neither of the maids can actually carry out the deed. Following through on a suggestion made earlier, we might postulate that it is because no true reciprocity exists between the servants and their mistress; they belong to a social hierarchy that inhibits direct action. In Girardian terms, the relevant social categories are still distinct enough to ward off the onset of violence.

The maids and their mistress are rivals in yet another obvious way, for they all desire Monsieur. The sisters' wish to replace Madame as Monsieur's lover is a constant source of tension and jealousy between them, as, e.g., when Claire accuses Solange of endangering their entire plan: " . . . toi, enivrée par le thème de ton amant coupable, criminel et banni, tu m'abandonnais" (p. 38). Less obviously, Claire and Solange may also, as in the previous trian-

gular relationships, desire to be the desired
object. In sexual terms, this would suggest
that, in order to possess the apparently heterosexual Madame, they would have to be men. But
it has a social meaning as well. Monsieur appears, after all, as the real (although absent)
figure of social authority, for it is the <u>bour-
geois</u>, not the <u>bourgeoise</u>, who can wield social
power. Women are traditionally excluded (and
even in Girard's theory, despite his token gesture toward feminism) from any active role in the
making of the cultural order. To have any real
position of strength in society, Claire and
Solange would have to be (like) Monsieur.

    These various relationships of rivalry
with Madame, while perhaps explaining the maids'
attempts to murder her, do not, however, explain the sisters' plot against Monsieur. What
would they gain by eliminating him? Here, by
continuing along the lines set forth immediately
above, we might postulate a mimetic relationship
in which the maids and Monsieur are rivals for
Madame. Solange and Claire, that is, in what
might seem a parody of the Oedipal scenario
(and yet a parody that may well reveal a better
understanding of women than either Freud or

Girard has demonstrated) would then appear as
a "band of sisters," eager to do away with the
father in order to possess the mother. "Vous
êtes un peu mes filles," says Madame after Monsieur has been put in jail, "Avec vous la vie
me sera moins triste. Nous partirons pour la
campagne. . . . A la campagne vous serez tranquilles. Je vous dorloterai" (p. 61).

  This attempt to apply Girard's concept
of "violent mimesis" to <u>Les Bonnes</u> must now
lead to a consideration of the scapegoating
mechanism that he sees as bringing the archaic
ritual to its conclusion. Girard's hypothesis
is that the sacrificial ritual commemorates an
originary act: the transfer of violence onto
a surrogate victim chosen by the community from
among its own members, yet not the party guilty
of the act that began the cycle of vengeance.
Henceforth, the sacrificial substitute will be
chosen from a group on the fringes of society
so as not to risk provoking a repeat of the
original blood feud. The rite then depends on
a distinction between the realm of the sacred
outside the community and the realm of the profane within; the scapegoat, however, must, by
definition, actively participate in both.[19] In

Les Bonnes, then, we must look for the substitute victim, not in the reality of the maids' social intercourse with their employer, but within their private ritual. We have seen that the maids' nightly ceremony is built upon the idea of a false Madame, or substitute monarch, replacing the "true" sovereign. Thus, it is "Madame" who will be punished for the transgressions, real or imaginary, of the patronne.

In Genet's play, however, this traditional formula has here too been modified, rendering the relationship sovereign/scapegoat more complex and ambiguous. Rather than simply a single focal point, the maids' rite has at least two. The exaltation of "Madame" is accompanied by the simultaneous degradation of the maids; the two cannot be separated. "Madame" exercises full authority over her servant, making her kneel, grovel, and submit to physical abuse, while the maids are debased, forced as they are to recall the midnight visits of the milkman and the odors of the belching sink.[20] The maids come to see themselves through what they assume to be the eyes of their mistress. Thus, speaking as Madame, Claire recites, as her own, what the sisters take to be society's estimation of the servile class.

> Je hais les domestiques. J'en
> hais l'espèce odieuse et vile.
> Les domestiques n'appartiennent
> pas à l'humanité. Ils coulent.
> Ils sont une exhalaison qui
> traîne dans nos chambres, dans
> nos corridors, qui nous pénètre,
> nous entre dans la bouche, qui
> nous corrompt. Moi, je vous
> vomis . . . Vos gueules d'épou-
> vante et de remords, vos coudes
> plissés, vos corsages démodés,
> vos corps pour porter nos dé-
> froques. Vous êtes nos miroirs
> déformants, notre soupape, notre
> honte, notre lie (pp. 82-3).

The maids, then, see themselves as the scapegoats of society, and indeed the marginal nature of servants has always made them a prime choice for the role of ritual victim.[21]

It is in this state of abjection that their revolt is born. "Nous sommes enveloppées, confondues dans nos exhalaisons, dans nos fastes, dans notre haine pour vous. Nous prenons forme" (p. 26). This is "le moment d'exhumer" (p. 17), bringing from the dead the now defiant maid. This is the moment in which Solange appears at last to "murder Madame," seeming to accomplish the deed she had many times attempted. In doing so, she enthrones herself; the maid-as-scapegoat is at last transfigured. "Je suis l'égale de Madame et je marche la tête haute . . . Maintenant j'ai ma robe rouge et je suis votre égale. Je porte la toilette rouge des criminelles" (p. 87). This is apparently the glory of the accomplished crime, of the daring transgression that, setting the étrangleuse apart from society, confers on her that sacred status previously reserved for Madame.

Yet, even now the exaltation is not, of course, complete, since the mock "Madame" has not actually been strangled at all. Determined, however, to realize their goal by truly destroying the sacred icon, Claire decides, as we have noted, to drink the poisoned tea herself. This act of self-sacrifice has the dual virtue of at once elevating Claire to the position of martyr and of enabling her sister to assume the glorious role of criminal in the eyes of the world.

Thus, there occurs at once the dethronement of a "Madame" and the enthronement of both maids: "Je grandis davantage pour te réduire et t'exalter" (p. 23).

This intended slaying of "Madame" may then be seen as the ritual murder of a sacrificial victim. There is, however, some uncertainty over which sister will dare the deed and face the consequences. Her own death will necessarily arise out of the circumstances of "Madame's" execution. At the same time, there is great rivalry between the sisters over who will play "Madame." The sisters appear to have agreed to take turns. One night Claire dressed in red assumes the role, the next night Solange dressed in white (p. 35). Nevertheless, the sisters do not always seem willing to follow their own conventions. Claire, for example, wants in the opening rite to wear Solange's ceremonial robe, not her own (pp. 16-18). (It might be said, then, that she wants to play Solange playing "Madame.") Later, when Solange attempts to strangle Claire, she puts on her ritual gown over her black maid's uniform, thus seeming intent on playing Madame even while playing the maid (p. 80ff). Girard suggests that the ritual dispute over the choice of the most suitable sacrifice is a displacement of the original reciprocal violence. The real question behind such preliminaries is, who will kill whom?[22]

How then can we explain the maids' seemingle contradictory (yet simultaneous) desires to be both victim and executioner, as well as the constant reversals and modifications of the ritual scenario this entails? Returning to the concept of violent mimesis, we find that both Claire and Solange desire to be the one to kill "Madame," i.e., to be the sacrificer. Since it is Solange who has tried to strangle Madame in profane time (p. 46), it will be Solange (as false Claire) who will try to strangle "Madame" during the ritual (pp. 26, 86). (Or perhaps Solange was only trying to act out in real life what she had attempted in a previous ritual enactment.) Similarly Claire, having failed to make Madame drink the poisoned tea in "reality" (pp. 51-3, 73-4), forces the false Claire "to make her" (as "Madame") drink the poisoned tea during the last ritual scene (pp. 92-3). Claire, then, appears to imitate her sister's desire for vengeance (at least in profane time), while Solange, playing her sister, must imitate Claire's

desire. At least, this seems the case at the
end of the second ritual enactment. Nevertheless, Solange, by following Claire's orders only accomplishes the crime(s) she has herself already long meditated: the murders of both "Madame" and Claire. It is, then, difficult to say exactly who is imitating whom, i.e., who has "originally" had which thoughts and desires or "originally" made which gestures. Nevertheless, the end result will be the elevation of Solange to the position of sacrificer even though this can only be accomplished through the cooperation of Claire who seems indeed to be committing suicide or sacrificing herself.

At the same time, however, the sisters are also rivals for the status of sacrificial victim. During the opening rite, Solange, as false Claire, takes upon herself the humiliation of the servant. And though it is not as servant, but as <u>étrangleuse</u>, that she envisions being executed, she does imagine herself on the way to the guillotine leading a parade of domestics, suggesting that it is perhaps also as maid (Pucelle?) that she is to die.

> On porte des couronnes, des fleurs,
> des oriflammes, des banderoles, on
> somme le glas. L'enterrement dé-
> roule sa pompe. Il est beau, n'est-
> ce pas? Viennent d'abord les maîtres
> d'hôtel, en frac, sans revers de soie.
> Ils portent leurs couronnes. Vien-
> nent ensuite les valets de pied, les
> laquais en culotte courte et bas
> blancs. Ils portent leurs couronnes.
> Viennent ensuite les valets de cham-
> bre, puis les femmes de chambre por-
> tant nos couleurs. Viennent les con-
> cierges, viennent encore les déléga-
> tions du ciel. Et je les conduis.
> Le bourreau me berce. On m'acclame.
> Je suis pâle et le vais mourir! (p. 89).

After having supposedly strangled "Madame" in the "second" ritual enactment, it is of her own sacrifice that she speaks in her grand soliloquy. But could she be both sacrificer and sacrificial victim? Solange, having in the ritual sacrificed her sister as "Madame," becomes a criminal in the eyes of society when she moves into the profane world. It is, however, important for her not to be completely guilty of the crime. (The scapegoat, according to Girard, is somewhat arbitrarily chosen.) It is not enough that "Madame" should not truly be dead. At the end of the play, we find Solange put in the role of murderer by her sister. She is, in other words, not completely guilty of the crime; it has chosen her. Nevertheless, Claire appears more clearly as the "innocent" sacrificial victim who dies in the place of another. She, in fact, sacrifices herself. As a result of this private execution, her sister, after having been exalted as sacrificer, will in turn be sacrificed as criminal. Each sister, then, is in turn and simultaneously, <u>criminelle</u> and <u>sainte</u>, sacrificer and sacrificed.

  Claire and Solange appear, therefore, as both models and rivals for the roles of sacrificial murderer and victim. Is there not perhaps a higher model? We have seen that they desire to be Monsieur, for he as <u>patron</u> has real authority. But is he a real <u>patron</u>? We **only** know that he is Madame's lover. Perhaps he is no more a genuine <u>bourgeois</u> than Madame a <u>bourgeoise</u>. Why then should the maids want to incriminate him? The maids' denunciation of Mon-

sieur, rather than just eliminating him from
the field of desire, has as <u>its goal his elevation to the position,</u> not of societal authority, but of <u>demi-monde</u> authority, i.e., to the
<u>position of great criminal</u>; they dream of mak-
ing him <u>un grand bagnard</u>. As such he would become an ideal/scapegoat model (<u>patron</u>) that Madame as well as her servants could emulate.
Consider that in the "Devil's Island story,"
each of the women casts herself in the role of
Faithful-Woman-Following-Her-Lover-Into-Torments.
They would like, in fact, to share his glory by
taking upon themselves his pains: "Tu étais
heureuse de ton sacrifice, de porter la croix
du mauvais larron, de lui torcher le visage, de
le soutenir, de te livrer aux chiourmes pour
que lui soit accordé un léger soulagement"
(p. 36).[23] The women, then, by making Monsieur
into a scapegoat, hope to put themselves in a
position to assume his role. This is the status
they seek by desiring to be Monsieur. Indeed,
when Claire has decided to poison Madame, it is
in the words of "Madame" (or are they Madame's?)
that she describes the journey of the convicted
murderer to Guyane, except that she puts herself
in the place of Monsieur: "Et s'il faut aller

plus loin, Solange, si je dois partir pour le bagne, tu m'accompagneras, tu monteras sur le bateau" (p. 49). The denunciation of Monsieur, even though it appears to fail (indeed, perhaps, as we shall see later, because it is intended to fail), still allows the maids to continue their ritual to the point at which they can assume the simultaneous, interinvolved roles of sacrificer and sacrificed; sacrificer because they have betrayed Monsieur, i.e., chosen him as victim, and sacrificed because they hope to follow and even replace him in this role as they construe it.

II.2   IM-PLICATIONS

We have thus seen how Genet modifies and complicates the pattern of primitive periodic ritual. Before going on to examine the implications of these alterations, we should consider the actual function of such rites in archaic societies. They appear to have been designed to ensure the continuance and prosperity of corporate life in all its manifestations. Consequently, their emphasis is generally upon the prosperity of society as a whole rather than upon the life and death of the individual. By

periodically re-enacting the creation of the
world out of chaos, the community seeks to re-
capture, according to Caillois, the vitality of
primordial forces or, according to Girard,
of those supposedly superhuman brings who first
imposed order. In either interpretation, the
old world is symbolically destroyed so that it
might be born again. Time is therefore circu-
lar, allowing, as it apparently does, for cyclical regeneration through the recovery of something like an absolute beginning.[24]

    There has, over the years, been a great
deal of debate about this putative <u>telos</u> of regeneration or renewal. Caillois has suggested
that periods of festive chaos may be necessary
to prevent the stagnation of an existing societal order. That order might thereby be strength-
ened, he believes, but without being altered in
any significant way. It would, on the contrary,
only have regained its full capacity to resist
the forces of change. Similarly, Girard, though
presenting a somewhat different view of violent
non-differentiation has nevertheless followed
Joseph de Maistre--the nineteenth century reac-
tionary theorist--in arguing that the ultimate
purpose of the ritual, and especially its sacrificial component, "is to restore harmony to the

community, to reinforce the social fabric." Thus, the ancient fête is frequently seen as an apparently radical means to an essentially conservatve end, viz., maintenance of the status quo. Hegel had already taken this position in his course on the philosophy of history, and anthropologists have generally echoed his view. They agree, as Nathalie Davis reports, that the ritualized communal activities of the ancient fête "are ultimately sources of order and stability in a hierarchical society."

> They can clarify the structure by the process of reversing it [she continues in her paraphrase of the conventional view]. They can provide an expression of, and a safety valve for, conflicts within the system. They can correct and relieve the systen when it has become arthoritarian. . . . [T]hey do not question the basic authority of the society itself. They can renew the system, but they cannot change it.

Davis herself does not agree, however, and she

is anticipated in this by Mikhail Bakhtin. Together they insist that, on the contrary, the old ritual festivities, instead of merely reinforcing institutions, may help to change them by providing experience of life with alternative values and hierarchies, as against the fixed categories of profane society. From this second perspective, the "carnivalization" of an established order may even suggest, as Dominick LaCapra points out, "a way in which institutions might be structured and yet allow if not encourage contestation, freedom, and play."[25]

If the purpose of the archaic periodic rite is to renew the social order, whether in a conservative or revolutionary sense, one might wonder about the purpose of Genet's rituals. Critics, like Richard Coe and Robert Brustein argue that, in the end, these private rituals merely repeat and therefore, in the conservative sense, "renew" existing structures of domination. In his theater, even the most overt rebellions are, they say, doomed by their tendency to mimic or re-present the established order.[26] Just as Claire and Solange re-enact the relationship between master and servant, so the revolutionaries in Le Balcon mimic great figures of society, the Blacks in Les Nègres the sterile sophistication of Whites, and the Arabs in Les Paravents the military organization of the French colonials. Thus, it would seem that, for Genet, the "changes" that do occur are only stages in a self-repeating cycle, and a cycle that inevitably reimposes the traditional values and norms. It might even be said with Girard as inspiration that his plays present scapegoating (e.g., of oppressed minorities like Blacks, Arabs, servants or criminals) as the necessary basis of any hierarchical ordering of society. Yet, none of his works present these values in an especially positive light, that society as vigorous and healthy, or its renewal as an occasion for rejoicing. In Les Bonnes, for example, cyclical repetition is treated in an apparently cynical fashion: the cycle only revives and perpetuates a highly undesirable order. Those critics, then, who conclude like Sartre that there is only sterile repetition in his theater will therefore generally be suggesting as well that Genet is either thoroughly antinomian or desperately pessimistic, and possibly both at once.[27]

Other critics who, like Jacques Ehrmann

and Lucien Goldmann, have dealt specifically
with the sociological implications of Genet's
theater, support this essentially negative
judgment by denying that the maids' ceremony
could have any effect at all on the society
that generates and regenerates it. They view
the personal ritual of Les Bonnes as simple
flights of fancy. At best it offers the protagonists a ludic escape by allowing them to act
out in fantasy possibilities that cannot be re-
alized in life, e.g., a slaughter of the ruling
class. Georges Bataille has gone even further
in his criticism of such solitary rites. Rather
than involving the whole community, the sacrifice of Claire and Solange appears to him an entirely private concern, the victims merely illu-
sory surrogates for particular individuals who
have provoked the sisters' anger. The latter
seem, then, to act solely for their own advan-
tage. Bataille, therefore, sees their supposed
"sacredness" as largely devoid of genuine significance. Like members of the funeral procession
in Pompes funèbres, they are alone, "capturés
dans un bloc de solitude": "Madame s'aperçoit
de ma solitude! Enfin! Maintenant je suis
seule! (p. 87). Confiscated from the community

by the solitary individual, such "sacredness," argues Bataille, represents the very denial of the purpose of the primitive rite. Girard, by contrast, identifies such individualization instead with a decadent stage in the evolution of sacrifice, a stage in which the sacrificial system has already begun to erode and a societal crisis looms up.

  The ways in which the traditional ritual pattern has been complicated by <u>Les Bonnes</u> might suggest, then, that more is at stake than the flight of a marginalized group, either through fantasy or ritual isolation, from a rigid hierarchical society. What this essay has described as the complexities or ambiguities of the play's ceremony might, were we to accept Girard's hypothesis, be seen as in fact characteristic of the failure of an entire sacrificial system. We would have before us, in other words, not a simply ritual representation of the sacrificial crisis, a representation that would end paradoxically in the reconfirmation and therefore renewal of an oppressive social order, but also, at the same time, a symptom of that very sacrificial crisis itself.

  Earlier we discussed the play in terms

of the relationships of violent reciprocity and
triangular desire that Girard suggests blur the
distinctions between characters. He might even
speak here of mirror images: Claire and Solange,
the false Claire (Solange) and Claire, the false
Madame (Claire) and Madame--the changing and
interchanging of roles does indeed become somewhat bewildering. For <u>Violence and the Sacred</u>,
the way out of such apparent chaos would then be
the sacrifice of a scapegoat. By violently establishing an arbitrary distinction between the
victim and the people, this ritual gesture would
forge the communal unanimity that can replace
the critical state of non-differentiation with
the foundation for a socially cohesive hierarchy
of distinctions. Paradoxically each member of
society would thereby seem as well to discover
and ground his own identity in and through the
sacrifice. We have seen, however, that <u>there is
always great continuity between victim and executioner in Les Bonnes. Indeed the roles so over-
lap that Claire and Solange may each play both,
in turn as well as simultaneously.</u> Girard explains that when there is too much continuity of
this sort there is great risk that "impure" profane violence begins to mingle with the "pure"

sacred violence of the rites as, e.g., in ordinary blood vengeance: "the elimination of violence is no longer effected; on the contrary, conflicts within the community multiply, and the menace of chain reactions looms ever larger."[28]

In <u>Les Bonnes</u>, the boundaries of sacred ritual and profane "reality" do indeed become blurred. After the alarm clock rings, for instance, ritual insults continue to flow into the now "profane" dialogue between the sisters. Madame's arrival and the ensuing conversation then replace the enthronement stage of the traditional ceremonial pattern. After Madam departs unharmed, "real" accusations exchanged by the sisters lead back into ritual insults. The status of this scene with the maids' employer discussed earlier is, therefore, particularly disturbing. In the terms of <u>Violence and the Sacred</u>, the maids have turned sacred violence into "a scandalous accomplice in the process of pollution, even a kind of catalyst in the propagation of further impurity."[29]

Turning then to the final scene, we find a dramatic example of what such "impurity" might be. The closing tableau represents a "sacred marriage" of sorts: "Ce couple éternal du criminel et de la sainte" (p. 49). (Here, as elsewhere, Genet creates a small but complex linguistic "carnival" of his own by playing—though it is play with a serious meaning as well, and as befits the carnival spirit—on the genders of French nouns. He makes one masculine and the other feminine, where "ordinarily" one would expect to find both nouns of the same gender—feminine in this case, though in general a masculine pair would be more "normal." By the same token, the present heterosexual coupling might easily be inverted, with the partners exchanging genders. It may also be the case that Solange is here also casting herself in the role of Monsieur and might consequently be called <u>le criminel</u>.) Solange, pretending to be handcuffed, but dressed now in white, is wedded to Claire "in death." From the "profane" perspective of normal society, however, this "marriage" can only appear monstrous because it is between individuals of the "same nature."[31]

      First, Claire and Solange are, of course, both women—sisters moreover. The ambiguity of the emotional relationship between them and the scenes of their mutual physical affection/abuse would seem to suggest a thrice illicit degree

of attraction between them: homosexual as well
as incestuous and sado-masochistic. Abnormalities of this sort were already suggested by our
earlier consideration of the possibilities inherent in the idea of violent mimesis and, indeed, sexual transgression has been identified
by Girard as a frequent aspect of the sacrificial crisis. When, for example, royal incest
is practiced (as it still is in parts of Africa) it plays a role in the sacred representations of that dangerous period of undifferentiation whose end is reenacted in the death of the
royal scapegoat. "L'homosexualité rituelle est
un phénomène assez fréquent," adds Girard in
Des choses cachées depuis la fondation du monde,
"elle se situe au paroxysme de la crise mimétique
et on la trouve dans des cultures qui ne font aucune place, semble-t-il, à l'homosexualité, en
dehors des rites religieux."[32]

Solange, le criminel, and Claire, la
sainte, are in addition not only siblings and
of the same sex, they are also both "sacred" figures. Sainteté and souillure--these are traditionally the two poles of the sacred and in many
cultures they are designated by the same term.[33]
When the Girardian sacrificial system works, an

arbitrary distinction is made between the two so that the "purity" of the saint, who transcends established laws, and the "impurity" of the criminal, who transgresses them, are felt to be entirely different. "As long as purity and impurity remain distinct," Girard maintains, "even the worst pollution can be washed away; but once they are allowed to mingle, purification is no longer possible."[34]

    For the crisis to come to an end, moreover, unanimous violence, on Girard's telling, would have to be directed against the sacrificial victim. He must be killed so that, through his death, violence might be redirected into constructive, society-enhancing channels. <u>Les Bonnes</u>, however, depicts no such moment of generalized, yet narrowly focused, destructiveness. No <u>patronne</u>, substitute or otherwise, ever appears to die. There is no decisive act of murder. Instead we have only the ambiguity of the drama's final tableau, therein it is never really clear whether at the curtain's fall Claire/"Madame" has finally been poisoned or whether this is yet another deceptive element of the ceremonial scenario. No one falls to the floor; in fact, we cannot even be sure the tea is "really" poisoned or is "actually" drunk. Consequently, the play might be seen as a displaced last supper or cène replete with "la profusion des ornements et des symboles." This highly problematic closing scene is, indeed, even less like a murder than that in which Solange appears to strangle her sister. The play seems, in other words, to have omitted any sacrifice or a ritual substitute; there seems to be no execution of a scapegoat.

The ritual has reached, then, no very certain conclusion with the final curtain, at least, no ultimate moment is ever actually made present. Nor, perhaps, is any such climax sought. The maids seem never to manage to go all the way. Their ritual foreplay is too long to allow "Madame" to die before Madame comes; Solange repeatedly fails to strangle her mistress in bed; the traces left by the maids announce Monsieur's release, causing Madame to withdraw too soon; even the expulsion of Monsieur is frustrated. It is almost as if the sisters desired to fail, desired never to be fully satisfied. It is as if what were exciting were the risks and dangers they run (e.g., by continuing the rite too close to the time of Madame's return, or denouncing

Monsieur, or pretending to court disaster):
"J'y suis plus belle! Le danger m'auréole
. . . " (p. 25). Perhaps the heightened stimulation and tension of unsatisfied desire is even itself the goal of their nightly ritual. Playing with death, in other words, may be more exciting than dying.

    The understanding of <u>Les Bonnes</u> from a Girardian perspective--though doubtless both possible and insightful--does not, however, seem entirely free of difficulties, some of them serious. The "sacrificial crisis" model is, up to a certain point, remarkably apt. Yet, in crucial respects, Genet's work cannot be confined nor perfectly comprehended within its inherent limitation. Girard's model would not, for example, appear adequately to account for either the complexities of the play's numerous and dynamically interrelating levels--narrative, dramatic, semantic, symbolic--or even for the ambiguities of its mimetic relationships. And this may well be because the play is in fact actively engaged in challenging the very concepts and relations between concepts that are fundamental to Girard's theory of sacrifice, principally his ideas of identity and mimesis.[35]

On Girard's hypothesis, all ritual, including Genet's, would be based on repetition, on "a sacred and immutable series of ceremonial gestures," to borrow Coe's phrase.[36] In <u>Les Bonnes</u>, however, we find neither pure repetition, nor, for that matter, total transformation. Instead, there are, as we have already noted at length, always a number of variations, never simply repeated, on a supposed "originary scene." Let us now only recall that, on what might be termed the paradigmatic level, the sisters, in their private ritual, imitate, or represent, the (idealized) "Madame," who imitates, or is derived from (but also exceeds) Madame, who in turn imitates, or conforms herself (somewhat imperfectly) to Monsieur or, rather, to her (more or less romanticized) impression of Monsieur and his way of life, all of which is again an imitation, or is based upon, the personality and behavior of the real Monsieur, whose precise nature and status (social, political, economic, erotic) is repeatedly, but in subtle ways, made to seem and left to remain, extremely uncertain and in fact suspicious. At the same time, however, it seems that Madame is also imitating, or attempting to achieve the stature of the model "Madame," who is imitating or designed largely in conformity with the maids' "forged" Monsieur, who is an imitation of a newspaper <u>bagnard</u>, and so on. All the characters are then cast, at one time or another, but also simultaneously, as sacrificial victim. On the syntagmatic level, we find several variant repetitions of the play's opening scene. The ritual's "second run-through," for example, is more complex and its tone more desperate, because the sisters fear discovery of their plot against their employer's lover. Two apparent murders occur, one again by strangulation, as in the "opening" rite, the other by poisoning as was attempted in "reality." There is also the added detail of a soliloquy in which Solange imagines (in this case a quite problematic form of anticipatory representation, itself already a problem for any theory of mimesis) her trial, her march to the guillotine, and Claire's funeral procession. The earlier ritual scenario has, in other words, been modified in significant ways. Instead, then, of true ritual cycles, we find in <u>Les Bonnes</u> a complex network of both differences within what appear to be repetitions of the same scenario, and repeated elements within what might seem to be rather different scenarios.

    Secondly, it has been noted that the primitive world-view envisions a periodic return to the beginning of time or of the world. According to Mircea Eliade, primitive man sees himself as a product of a sacred history. He is obliged to know, and regularly to repeat, what his superhuman forefather did <u>initio</u> <u>et</u> <u>ab</u> <u>origine</u>. By re-enacting the creation, the primitive re-presents a fantastic world-scenario that has "disappeared." This primary archetypal scene or Great Original which critics like Sartre or Coe see as bestowing meaning on Genet's theatrical gestures is, however, according to Girard's hypothesis, merely a myth that replaces the original act of scapegoating actually performed by the unanimous group. The primitive "ritual system" is, then, an attempt to reproduce an original event that actually took place, to recover the unanimity that occurred and recurred around the person of the surrogate victim. It is, in Girardian terms, a reenactment of the emergence of the social order out of the state of undifferentiated nature.[37]

    But to what origin do the maids ever return? When the curtain rises, the ceremony has already begun, and clearly not for the first time. When the maids take up the rite again after Madame's departure, "les formalités du début" (p. 81) are explicitly set aside. The rite never really starts; it is always already in progress.

The fact that the maids do not ever begin their ritual "at the beginning" may not seem sufficient to cast the existence of such a beginning into doubt. We should therefore consider what would in fact be required in order to constitute such an original scene. Continuing to employ the Girardian model, we would expect the maids' nightly ceremony to repeat, through ritual substitution, the sacrifice of an original scapegoat, here an archetypal Madame. The latter would then in turn represent the "first" surrogate victim whose death permitted the establishment of the cultural order. We might expect that the crucial role of the archetypal victim in "the originary scene" would be filled by the maid's employer. We have noted, however, that the patronne is in this case already a mere imitation and not the genuine maîtresse bourgeoise. She herself is copying the behavior of an imagined archetype. She is, in other words, already a substitute. The false Madame of the maids' rite is then a substitute for a substitute. The problem is compounded, however, by the fact that, alternatively, Madame's role will occasionally appear to "borrow" certain elements from the ritual of her domestics. Who, for instance, "created" the story of following one's lover to Devil's Island, "Madame" (p. 18), or Madame (p. 56)? In general, it is the supposedly "false" figure who appears first and introduces us to the character and behavior of the "real" Madame. A similar questioning of "originary mimesis" can be found in Le Journal du voleur. There, the narrator tells us he appropriated the gestures, words and voice of his friend, Stilitano. Stilitano himself, however, was only trying to imitate "un héros idéal, le Stilitano dont l'image était déjà inscrite dans un ciel de gloire." The entire series of imitations is then rendered suspect when the narrator reveals that Stilitano "était ma propre création."[38] The narrator, it seems, is imitating the criminel he has himself created. Similarly, if Madame as substitute victim is a copy of the ritual "Madame," who is herself a fiction created by the sisters, then the existence of anything like an original scene is cast rather thoroughly into doubt.

It might be said, however, that we have failed to take sufficiently into account one of the participants in this ritual play. If Madame/ "Madame" is to be seen as a substitute sacrificial victim for an "original" surrogate <u>patronne</u>, for whom is this latter a replacement? Girard has wondered whether "the preponderance of women" in certain myths and tragedies "does not constitute a secondary mythological displacement, an effort to exonerate from the accusation of violence, not mankind as a whole, but adult males, who have the greatest need to forget their role in the crisis because, in fact, they must have been largely responsible for it." The primal male community, then, wishing to pass blame onto a generalized scapegoat, chose women "by reason of her weakness and relatively marginal social status."[39] It is as if the guilty sovereign, seeking a victim to take his place, chose his queen. In <u>Les Bonnes</u>, the Great Original or "primary" surrogate, for whom the archetypal <u>patronne</u> could be called a subsequent substitute might then appear the archetypal <u>patron</u>. Just as there appears to be no true Madame, however, there may be no true Monsieur, for there is some doubt as to the exact socio-economic status of Madame's lover. More significant, however, is the image of Monsieur created by the maids' treachery. Through their forgeries, he becomes a criminal in the eyes of the law; falsely accused, we might call him, too, a scapegoat. Having once acquired this status, he may, as we have seen, serve as a model for the maids' own self-sacrifice. As in the case of Stilitano, the criminal-as-scapegoat whom the maids attempt to imitate turns out to be their own "creation," cobbled together out of accounts the sisters have read, both fiction (stories from Détective) and factual (proceedings of the Cour d'assises) plus their first-hand experience of denouncing (actually of framing) Madame's paramour (pp. 69, 58). There does not, therefore, appear ever to have been a real "first" surrogate victim; in Les Bonnes there are always only substitutes. The sacrifice of the original surrogate seems merely a retrospective postulate or, as Hayden White has called it, a "mythical truth."[40]

The possibility, or even likelihood, of an endless series of substitutions without anchor in an original, hence creative, act has serious implications, not only for Girard's theory in particular, but also for the archaic ritual pattern in general. The impossibility of ever locating an originary scene of course casts doubt upon its empirical existence. Yet we must agree with Girard that an hypothesis like his (or Freud's for that matter) does not require empirical confirmation to be a useful means of understanding certain phenomena or aspects of them. Nevertheless, Girard explicitly refuses to call his hypothesis a necessary explanatory fiction. He claims, on the contrary, that the original crisis must have historical reality: ". . . the structuring power of real victimage is the only means to make complete sense, not of the collective violence alone, but of all the other features as well, the one and only solution that brings to mythology the kind of coherent intelligibility no rational mind can disguise."[41]

More interesting for our discussion of the ritual in *Les Bonnes*, however, is Girard's assertion that this primal scene is outside the pale of representation. Furthermore, he insists "that it is possible to return to the hither side of [en deçà de] represented mimesis, that is, to the near or prior side of the sacrificial (ritual) 'imitation' of the primitive murder."

This is because, continuing Phillippe Lacoue-Labarthe's paraphrase of Girard, "mimesis in general, beginning with that in which reciprocal violence (namely desiring mimesis itself) takes root, is anterior, in some way or another, to representation."[42]

> Ce que désir "imite", ce qu'il emprunte à un "modèle", en deçà des gestes, des attitudes, des manières, de tout ce à quoi on réduit toujours la mimésis en ne l'appréhendant jamais qu'au niveau de la représentation, c'est le désir lui-même, sur un mode d'une immédiateté quasi osmotique, forcément trahie et perdue dans toutes les dualités des problématiques modernes du conscient et de l'inconscient.[43]

Such an appeal to a realm outside representation--hence, outside language in general, however broadly understood--even when, as in Girard's case, it takes the form of a "scientific" postulat that conflictual mimesis exists in the animal realm where it precedes representations and every system of signs in any sense links Girard's theory closely with the dominant, onto-theological tradition of the West with its search for totalization and oneness.[44] Language creates and requires the distance--e.g., between word and referent, signified and signifier, <u>destinateur</u> and <u>destinataire</u>--that make communication both possible and necessary at all. Outside of language, in a realm of pure "immediateness," there would be no distance whatever between what perceives and that which is perceived. Thus, there would be difference between word and referent, signified and signifier, <u>destinateur</u> and <u>destinataire</u>. There would also be no difference between individual and model. It is difficult, therefore, to see how anything like mimesis or desire--much less mimetic desire--could exist or even be possible in such a state of pure identity. It does not, in fact, seem too much to say that the state of absolute immediateness is simply not compatible with the existence of a world in any sense. Indeed, such a state cannot even be very readily imagined.

    The absence of any clearly originary scene in <u>Les Bonnes</u>, like the absence of ultimate closure or pure repetition, has, therefore, still further implications for Girard's conception of mimetic ritual, for it leads to the more general philosophical problem of identity. Recent developments in continental thought have involved the attempt to demonstrate the relation of this fundamental concept to the dominant ontological tradition in the West, a tradition rooted in what has been called a "metaphysics of presence." Girard specifically relates mimesis to the problem of being in his discussion of desire:

> Once his basic needs are satisfied (indeed sometimes even before), man is subject to intense desires, though he may not know precisely for what. The reason is that he desires <u>being</u>, something he himself lacks and which some other person seems to possess. The subject thus looks to that other person to inform him of what he should desire in order to acquire that being. If the model, who is apparently al-

>ready endowed with superior be-
>ing, desires some object, that
>object must surely be capable
>of conferring an even greater
>plenitude of being.[45]

On this telling, Claire and Solange would, as Coe has already argued, "become what-they-are by imitating the gesture of [the] archetype, by becoming somebody else."[46] Historically, moreover, "to be" has been understood as "to have presence in the moment that now is." Only insofar as it "now is" has existence been considered "actual." Only insofar as an entity "presents" itself has it been said that it truly "is." Being, then, has come to mean "presence."[47]

Through its complex interplay of presence and absence, however, Les Bonnes appears to call this very conception into question. In the play, for example, the archetypal maîtresse bourgeoise is always absent, an idealized fiction. Yet, insofar as she constantly informs the behavior of each character, Madame-the-ideal is, at the same time, always in some sense present. Similarly, the maids' employer--herself merely a self-styled and only partially successful imitation of this archetype--although she is never physically part of the maids' ceremony, is, for the maids, nevertheless always "present" to a certain extent--a living symbol, as it were, of the ideal Madame. She too, then, can be a constant presence of sorts, while yet remaining physically offstage for most of the play. This problem of absence and presence is yet more complex, however, in that the maids' *patronne*-- when she is physically absent--is replaced, for the time of the ritual, by one of the sisters. Claire playing "Madame" is hence, and as we have noted, actually a substitute for an already substitute Madame. In this way, a representation of the ideal will always be physically "present" during the ritual. And Claire--in her capacity as the "representation"--herself will simultaneously be absent as well. She can, of course, never be completely "Madame." But neither can she be completely herself as she plays at "representing" the ideal Madame. She is constantly vacillating between the two--sometimes playing one, sometimes the other, most often both at once. No substitute--whether the character Madame or Claire--is, in the end, ever entirely present, nor, by the same token, ever completely absent. Therefore, not only is there never any genuine (i.e., original) Surrogate Victim, there is never even the same substitute for long. Neither is the substitute fixed within itself--Claire plays both "Madame" and herself. The maids' ritual cannot generate the traditional cycles of repetition because its elements are always in a state of flux. Nothing is ever consistent with itself, nor simply transformed into a stable embodiment of anything else.

In <u>Les Bonnes</u>, then, presence and absence exist simultaneously in a tensely involved relationship, always overlapping but without being sublated into a higher unity or dichotomized into a pure opposition. The entire nature of the maids' rite, in other words, is ultimately somewhat ambiguous. Girard would probably reject this view as a product of faulty reasoning. "When we speak of ambivalence [or ambiguity-- he does not seem to distinguish between them] we are," he writes, "only pointing to a problem that remains to be solved," to a "perfectly decipherable message" that one has so far simply failed or refused to decipher.[48] It appears from the overall argument of <u>Violence and the</u>

Sacred that the "underlying unity" of, in this case, the sacred, should enable us "to bring together all the disparate elements . . . into an intelligible whole."[49] For, as Girard will explain, genuine ambivalence or ambiguity is nothing but a manifest logical absurdity, since two contradictory or opposing elements cannot exist in the same time/space without destroying the axiomatic unity of that time/space. This would, of course, seem to mean Girard has in fact begun by begging the entire question. Having first rejected ambiguity--the existence of (more or less) incompatible elements or aspects within the same time/space--as impossible per definitionem, however, Girard's ritual theory will subsequently be unable to deal satisfactorily with the intricacies of a play like Les Bonnes, i.e., of a work that stages the sustained interrogation of precisely this traditional assumption of identity and difference upon which that theory appears to rely.

Accordingly, ambivalence or ambiguity described on the first page of Violence and the Sacred as essentially an error of logic and hence a delusion--the dangerous offspring and prop of feeble reasoning--is promptly expelled from the Girardian hypothesis of generative violence. Its place is then taken by a substitute, similar yet distinct enough to be more easily managed: the chaotic non-differentiation of, for example, the sacrificial crisis.[50]

The problem of ambivalence or ambiguity, "solved" by and then excluded from Girard's hypothesis, apparently returns in the end, however, to occupy a central position in the ritual, for the scapegoat itself is a thoroughly ambiguous figure: simultaneously guilty and innocent, inside the social order as well as outside. Indeed, even for Girard, "he partakes of all possible differences within the community."[51] Lacoue-Labarthe has, moreover, noted that the traditional pharmakos, because of its "pure and disquieting plasticity which authorizes potentially the changing appropriation of all the characters and all the functions (all the roles)," because of its "typical virtuosity," because it is "without any other property than an infinite malleability: instability 'itself,'" because, in other words, it incarnates "the general absence of identity or rather . . . the primitive native default of identity"--for all these reasons, the scapegoat must be eliminated in order that propriety and order can be (re)instituted.[52]

The scapegoat mechanism, however, is designed to expell not only that ambiguous creature, but also a far more immediately dangerous force: violence itself. And it is a force that is no less problematic. "At once seductive and terrifying," it is also simultaneously beneficent and malificent. According to the Girardian hypothesis, the distinction between "good" and "evil" violence is an arbitrary one. Nevertheless, it is perceived as fundamental; it must be made in order to protect the human community from its own violent nature. "Evil" violence then becomes that reciprocal hostility that "divides, destroys, and levels," causing a general loss of differentiation (including, as we have seen, the loss of the distinction between "pure" and "impure" violence). "Good" violence, on the other hand, is perceived as that unanimous (i.e., sacrificial) violence that "regulates, pacifies and reconciles." It appears, in fact, almost homeopathic in that a "small" act of violence directed against a surrogate victim replaces the large-scale bloodletting of generative violence. By purging hostility in this way, it keeps it in check. Such preventative violence is deemed beneficent because it is said to maintain the sacrificial system and hence the community in existence.[53]

Nevertheless, this sacrificial violence is itself highly problematic, for although it is not identical to those other forms of "impure" violence, it is still quite similar.[54] In the Girardian hypothesis, as we saw above, it appears positive, in that it leads to the possibility of culture. Yet, it is not simply positive since it is still somewhat destructive. The execution of the scapegoat, as a form of murder, reminds society that its own violence is ever present and consequently must be contained within the "rigorously determined forms" of ritual practice.[55] Even such restricted forms of violence, however, should eventually be eliminated along with the sacrificial system itself. This is the function Girard attributes to Christianity in <u>Des choses cachées depuis la fondation du monde</u>. There he asserts that the Crucifixion brings an end to the sacrificial system, so that violent unanimity may give way to peaceful union in Christ.[56]

By driving out this paradoxical force--and to violence we might also add the sacred[57]--

society as well as all its cultural forms, including perhaps even our familiar forms of logic, affirms internal identity in addition to external difference. It establishes, that is, those clear and distinct categories of thought that make ambiguity appear a scandal for thinking or even altogether impossible. Thus, it would seem that ambiguity itself--as the possibility of less than perfect self-identity, of less than absolute differences--is in a sense (and perhaps more than one) the ultimate scapegoat of <u>Violence</u> <u>and</u> <u>the</u> <u>Sacred</u>.

The scapegoat, however, is more than a bearer of ambiguity or undecidability. It is also the "representative of mimesis." For, as Plato suggests in <u>The</u> <u>Republic</u>, and as Lacoue-Labarthe reminds us, the possibility of mimesis supposes a lack of being-proper, a basic im-propriety. Mimesis therefore appears to Plato as "the <u>unassignable</u> danger" of an "originary absence of subjective 'property.'"[58] It is paradoxical, then, that Girard should consider full "being" the ultimate goal of the mimetic rivalry, since imitation or representation appears the most profound and all pervasive inhibition necessarily to affect every quest for that state of ontological fulfillment or perfection. Indeed this is perhaps the reason he insists, as we saw, that it exists already in a time before representation and hence, before all distance-- a pre-lapsarian state--understandably rather difficult to describe or depict, in which being is always immediately present to itself, at least "quasi-osmotically." Nevertheless, as our discussion of the problematic "origin" of the maids' ritual has attempted to demonstrate, the empirical nature of mimesis also points to what Lacoue-Labarthe has signalled as the "danger" that "representation might be primal." The Girardian ritual hypothesis, then, by attempting to eliminate undecidability in a move to the prior side of representation--toward absolute (self-)presence--may well be trying to do away with mimesis itself.[59]

Les Bonnes, however, by refusing to establish any clear distinction, e.g., between presence and absence, sacred and profane, male and female, sacrificer and sacrificed, Solange and Claire, Madame and "Madame," etc., questions the very need for the scapegoat mechanism and through that mechanism the logic of identity and difference. At the same time, the complexities of its ceremonial scenarios suggest an understanding of the "essence" of mimesis as the infinity of substitution and circulation, and therefore, an understanding of the problems of those traditional concepts of imitation and repetition, said by theorists like Girard to inform the archaic ritual patterns. Indeed the play goes even further, suggesting that the ambiguities and complexities which, according to at least the Girardian hypothesis, archaic societies would perceive as monstrous, might even be provocative and stimulating in a positive sense, and hence, in this sense, creative.

This discussion of the relationship between <u>Les Bonnes</u> and archaic ritual, with particular reference to the model of the latter described in <u>Violence and the Sacred</u>, has attempted to show how Genet's dramatic work, by modifying certain aspects of the traditional rite, destabilizes the cyclical world-view on which that rite is based. Certain important elements of this destabilizing impetus will now reappear as we turn to the other basic ritual pattern with which Genet's theater plays: the Christian or transcendent.

NOTES

¹ James George Frazer, The New Golden Bough, ed. T. Gaster (New York: New American Library, 1964), pp. 273-338. Emile Durkheim, The Elementary Forms of the Religious Life, trans. J. W. Swain (1915; rpt. New York: Free Press, 1965), p. 391; see also Dominick LaCapra, Emile Durkheim: Sociologist and Philosopher (Ithaca, N.Y.: Cornell University Press, 1972), pp. 209-11.

² Frazer suggested that the king was executed because he had lost his strength and virility (pp. 275-80). Girard calls this theory fanciful, a tardy afterthought. He believes that the king, like Oedipus, was originally accused of some horrible crime in order that the community might unite against him, thus channeling reciprocal violence onto a single individual (pp. 106-7). Jean Pierre Vernant in "Ambiguité et renversement" shows that in the works of Homer and Hesiod the king is executed because he has faltered in the dispensing of justice, bringing down misfortune on the entire society (quoted in Girard, p. 97n).

³ Girard, pp. 105, 107.

⁴ Jean Genet, Les Bonnes et Comment jouer Les Bonnes (Décines: L'Arbalète, 1963), p. 22. All future references to this work will be given in the body of the text.

⁵ Genet added the notation "Solange (comme en adoration)" to the second version of the play. This revision also makes the distance between the maid and her mistress appear insuperable: "Les frontières ne sont pas des conventions, mais des lois. Ici mes terres, la votre rivage" (Sceaux: J.J. Pauvert, 1954), pp. 93-4.

⁶ Emile Benveniste, Problèmes de linguistique générale (Paris: Gallimard, 1966), p. 228.

⁷ Zimbardo, pp. 249-50; Jean Genet, Le Journal du voleur (Paris: Gallimard, 1949), p. 22.

⁸ Girard, pp. 39, 272.

⁹ Roger Caillois, L'Homme et le sacré, 2ᵉ édition (Paris: Gallimard, 1950), pp. 135ff.

¹⁰ Caillois, p. 158; see also Nathalie Z. Davis, Society and Culture in Early Modern France (Stanford: Stanford University Press, 1975), p. 129. Girard, p. 141.

¹¹ Jean Genet, Notre Dame des Fleurs, in his Oeuvres complètes II (Paris: Gallimard, 1951), p. 119. For a more complete discussion

see Sartre, pp. 561-5. Tom O'Horgan actually staged <u>Les Bonnes</u> with actors playing the roles of Claire and Solange in October, 1964. This New York City production is reviewed in "<u>The Maids</u> Performed by Men," <u>The Theater of Jean Genet: A Casebook</u>, ed. Richard Coe (New York: Grove Press, 1970), pp. 58-60.

[12] Girard, p. 119; Frazer, p. 642; Mikhail Bakhtin, <u>Problems of Dostoevski's Poetics</u>, trans. R. W. Rostel (Ann Arbor: Ardis, 1973), p. 101.

[13] Sartre, p. 567.

[14] Girard, pp. 145-7.

[15] Sartre, pp. 570-1.

[16] Genet, "Comment jouer <u>Les Bonnes</u>," p. 8. Furthermore, the sustained image here is one of male homosexuality.

[17] Genet, "Comment jouer," p. 11.

[18] Girard, pp. 146, 147.

[19] Girard, pp. 102, 271.

[20] Zimbardo, p. 249.

[21] Girard, p. 12. Here we might do well to recall Genet's words of warning to those who would turn his play into a plea for oppressed minorities: ". . . il ne s'agit pas d'un plaidoyer sur le sort des domestiques. Je suppose

qu'il existe un syndicat des gens de maison--
cela ne nous regarde pas"("Comment jouer," p. 11).

22 Girard, p. 124.

23 It is noteworthy that in their Devil's
Island fantasy," the maids choose to describe
themselves as a Simon who helps, neither Christ,
nor the Good Thief, but rather the mauvais larron. They choose in imitate, in other words,
a "bad" substitute.

24 Caillois, pp. 23, 123, 140; René Girard, "Interview," Diacritics, March 1978), p.
391. Cf. Mircea Eliade, Aspects du mythe (Paris:
Gallimard, Collection "Idées," 1963), pp. 24-5,
43-4 and Mikhail Bakhtin, Rabelais and His World,
trans. Helene Iswolsky (Cambridge, Mass.: M.I.T.
Press, 1968), pp. 1-58.

25 G.W.F. Hegel, The Philosophy of History, trans. J. Sibrie (New York: Dover Publi-
cations, Inc., 1956), pp. 54, 72; see also Girard, Violence, pp. 92, 8, 280. David, p. 130;
see also Mircea Eliade, Le Mythe de l'éternel
retour: Archetypes et répétitions (Paris: Gallimard, Collection "Idées," 1949), p. 134.
Davis, pp. 97, 119, 123, 131. Dominick LaCapra,
A Preface to Sartre (Ithaca, N.Y.: Cornell University Press, 1978),p. 27.

[26] Richard Coe, The Vision of Jean Genet (London: Peter Owen, 1968), p. 258; Robert Brustein, The Theater of Revolt: An Approach to Modern Drama (Boston: Little, Brown, and Co., 1964), p. 394. Sartre, p. 309.

[27] Jacques Ehrmann, "Genet's Dramatic Metamorphosis: From Appearance to Freedom," Yale French Studies, No. 29 (Spring-Summer, 1962), pp. 33-42; Lucien Goldmann, "The Theater of Genet: A Sociological Study," The Theater of Jean Genet: A Casebook, ed. R. N. Coe (New York: Grove Press, 1970), pp. 220-238. Jean Genet, Pompes funèbres, in his Oeuvres complètes III (Paris: Gallimard, 1953), p. 140; cf. "J'ai atteint une solitude me conférant la souveraineté." Le Journal du voleur, pp. 184-5. Georges Bataille, La Littérature et le mal (Paris: Gallimard, 1957), pp. 224, 226; Girard, p. 101.

[28] Girard, p. 39.

[29] Ibid.

[30] A still better example of language making greater allowance for sexual inversion or role reversal than society "normally" does-- of a language, perhaps, that would appear able to function in some still entirely licit ways as, in a sense, the carnivalesque double of mun-

dane society--is the phrase "les brûlantes amours de la sentinelle et du mannequin," attributed to Genet by Sartre in "Plaidoyer pour les intellectuels," Situations VIII (Paris: Gallimard, 1972), p. 435.

[31] Caillois, p. 103.

[32] Girard, p. 104-6; Des choses cachées depuis la fondation du monde, with J.-M. Oughourlian and Guy Lefort (Paris: Bernard Grasset, 1978), p. 359.

[33] The Latin sacer, for example, is sometimes translated sacred, sometimes accursed, for its range of significatory power encompasses both the maleficent and the beneficent. Caillois, pp. 39-40; Girard, Violence, p. 259. See also Sigmund Freud, "The Antithetical Sense of Primal Words," in Character and Culture, ed. R. Rieff (1963; rpt. New York: MacMillan Publishing Co., Collier Books, 1978), pp. 34-43.

[34] Girard, Violence, p. 38.

[35] For a brief but highly suggestive treatment of this problem in the context of the relationship between Sartre and Genet, see LaCapra, Preface, pp. 179-83.

[36] Coe, pp. 43, 274.

[37] Eliade, Aspects du mythe, pp. 24-5;

Girard, Violence, pp. 276, 167. Coe, 43; Sartre, pp. 298-9. Cf. the Last Supper which was itself both a last mass and a first mass commemorated in later masses -- both a "closure" and, simultaneously, an "origin."

38 Genet, Le Journal, pp. 191, 133, 136.

39 Girard, Violence, pp. 139, 141.

40 Hayden White, "Ethnological 'Lie' and Mythical 'Truth.'" Diacritics (March 1978), pp. 2-9.

41 Girard, "Interview," p. 41.

42 Phillippe Lacoue-Labarthe, "Mimesis and Truth," Diacritics (March 1978), p. 17.

43 René Girard, "Système du délire," Critique, No. 306 (November 1972), p. 963. This use of the phrase en deçà de ("hither side") is somewhat confusing at first, since from the context one would expect au delà de ("thither side"). Girard seems here not to be speaking from the position of modern culture at all, but rather from a position on the other side of representation, i.e., a position prior to man's fall into language, however broadly understood. He then would seem to be looking at us from across the lapsus, as it were. Consequently, he appears implicitly to be claiming to have attained him-

self that state of "quasi-osmotic immediateness" (analogous to the mystic's relation to the deity).

[44] Girard, "Interview," p. 34.
[45] Girard, Violence, p. 146.
[46] Coe, p. 45.
[47] Martin Heidegger, Being and Time, trans. J. Macquarrie and E. Robinson (New York: Harper and Row, 1962), pp. 47, 425-6.
[48] Girard, Violence, pp. 1, 182. It seems that Girard here begins himself to collapse or blur some rather important distinctions. He begins, that is, to confuse the existence of genuine problems, to borrow a distinction argued for by Dominick LaCapra, (like the nature of being or of the sacred) with that of mere puzzles. The first have been an almost constant source and focus of anxious speculation, not so much because of their admitted complexity, but rather because of their inherent and irreducible ambiguities, their capacity for provoking an ambivalent response. History has never "resolved" such genuine problems. On the contrary, each new age must raise and confront them yet once again. The puzzle, by contrast, gives way in the end. It yields to rational, scientific,

hence <u>technological</u> solutions. The puzzle has
a (more or less) definitive answer, and does not
trouble human history past a certain point. The
basic elements of every science are the puzzles
we have solved. Cf. Hayden White's "Ethnological 'Lie" and Mythical 'Truth'" for a somewhat
different but related criticism of what Girard
has called the "scientific" nature of his "solution" to the cultural problem. Thus, in the domain of ethnology, for example, it has long been
recognized that the category of the sacred involves the invocation of order as well as disorder, peace as well as war, creation as well as
destruction. Initially, both implicitly and explicitly he maintains that <u>Violence and the Sacred</u> has at last resolved them.

[49] Girard, <u>Violence</u>, p. 258.

[50] Girard, <u>Violence</u>, p. 23. Girard effects this substitution in different ways. On
the one hand, he denies that two things actually
occurring in the same time/space can really be
different. He eliminates, that is, any apparent
distinctions between them, insisting that those
perceived are in fact only "functional" or "mythical," and ultimately not genuine at all (p. 25).
On the other, where the first tactic will not

work (often because the entities in question are simply too different) he denies they actually occur in the same time/space. Instead they are said to oscillate or alternate in occurrence, being involved, as they seem to him, only in reciprocity, "revolving oppositions," "violent mimesis," the "double bind of imitated desires." This second tactic begins to look surprisingly like the first, however, when Girard asserts that although the oscillating elements appear different to someone within the system, they are "ultimately indistinguishable" to the objective observer without. Paradoxically, this general objective lack of distinction--though it might (if demonstrable) enable Girard to resolve ambivalence or ambiguity into non-differentiation --is itself generally described elsewhere as the hallmark of that sacrificial or "identity" crisis which repeatedly threatens the very existence of society in the modern age: "In this situation no one and nothing is spared; coherent thinking collapses and rational activities are abandoned. All associative forms are dissolved or become antagonistic; all values, spiritual or material, perish" (pp. 51, 149-50, 158-9). Indeed, it is during this crisis that the false distinctions traditionally perceived by ethnologists (as well

as by certain modern philosophers and literary
critics) break down, finally revealing a fundamental lack of genuinely clear and valid categories. Familiar ambiguities stand revealed at
last as what they are: simple confusion or self-
delusion, that encourages the rising tide of con-
ceptual and ultimately social chaos, rather than
holding it back as firm and clear-cut distinctions would. According to Girard, the way to
bring such a large-scale cultural crisis to an
end is by violently (hence, firmly) establishing
at least one distinct difference. The selection
of the scapegoat arbitrarily draws precisely
this sort of distinction between the community
and the sacrificial victim. At bottom, of course,
it too is ultimately a false differentiation but
so long as this "subversive" truth (p. 318) remains concealed, the scapegoat's death can bring
the critical state of non-differentiation to an
end. The tensions that radical difference pro-
vokes are then transcended through the scapegoat's
expulsion or execution, so that a higher communal
unity may be attained. Founded in violence the
latter is then solid enough to replace the non-
differentiaion of the sacrificial crisis.

    51 Girard, *Violence*, p. 271.

[52] Lacoue-Labarthe, p. 20.

[53] Girard, Violence, pp. 152, 115-16, 58, 114, 8.

[54] See Girard, Violence, p. 2: "If sacrifice resembles criminal violence, we may say that there is, inversely, hardly any form of violence that cannot be described in terms of sacrifice. . . . [S]acrifice and murder would not lend themselves to this game of reciprocal substitution if they were not in some way related."

[55] Girard, Violence, pp. 110, 99.

[56] Girard, Choses cachées, p. 204ff.

[57] See Girard, Violence, p. 258: "I have used the phrase 'violence and the sacred'; I might as well have said 'violence or the sacred.' For the operations of violence and the sacred are ultimately the same process."

[58] Lacoue-Labarthe, p. 20.

[59] Ibid.

III   SACRAMENTAL ELEVATION

Initially, this essay envisioned the Christian and primitive conceptions of ritual as alternatives, and even largely contradictory. Nevertheless, it seems this apparent opposition cannot really be sustained, despite Girard's assertion of a radical break between archaic sacrifice and Christianity.[1] Christian ceremonies are not entirely free from the traces of older rites, while certain pagan mystery cults were already in some ways transcendent. The two types of ritual, then, seem neither clearly distinct nor ever fully identical. The Catholic Mass may borrow from and, to a degree, incorporate many elements of more primitive ritual practice, though a great deal is always left out in the process. And, of course, a great deal is added as well.

The Mass, then, is not simply sacrifice, but also sacrament; not only cyclical re-enactment, but also transcendent union or, more precisely, substantial transformation. In the mystery of the Eucharist, the Host, or consecrated wafer of bread, and the chalice of wine, contain <u>vere</u>, <u>realiter</u>, <u>substantialiter</u>, the body and

blood of Christ. The believer who receives the
Host in communion partakes of the divine and
universal <u>individuum</u>. This is the doctrine of
the Real Presence. The entire substance of the
bread has been converted into the Body of Christ
and the entire substance of the wine into His
Blood; only the appearances of bread and wine,
their accidents, remain: "Sous les apparences
les plus familières--une croûte de pain--on y
dévore un dieu."[2]

    The fact that the substance of Christ is
believed to be "contained within," "kept together
with" ($<$ <u>contineo</u>, to be enclosed in, to be surrounded by) the accidental appearance of the wafer might lead to the perception of a seemingly
analogous "sacramental quality" in Genet's ritual: the superimposition of "opposites"--e.g.,
servant/master, criminal/saint, real/artificial
objects, realistic movement/ritualistic gesture
--and their apparent <u>Aufhebung</u> in a consecrating
movement. The spectator notices the interinvolvement of images when words that belong to one element of the opposition show up in the speech of
the other. Claire (as false Madame) speaks in
an ironic tone, for instance, to Solange (who
plays Claire).

> Evitez de me frôler. Reculez-
> vous. Vous sentez la fauve.
> De quelle infecte soupente où
> la nuit les valets vous visi-
> tent rapportez-vous ces odeurs?
> La soupente! La chambre des
> bonnes! La mansarde! C'est
> par mémoire que je parle de
> l'odeur des mansardes, Claire.
> Là . . . Là, les deux lits de
> fer séparés par la table de
> nuit (p. 19).

Yet, Madame never enters the maids' quarters; rather, it is Claire's personal bitterness that shows here through her role. Similarly, the story of the milkman, to which the ritual repeatedly alludes, is a detail from the maids' profane life. Moving in the other direction, ceremony may also penetrate into "reality," as in Claire's reactions to the distribution of Madame's old wardrobe. The red velvet dress and the fur stole ("le manteau de parade") are still sacred garments, always to be touched only with trepidation: "Jamais je n'oserai la mettre. Elle est si belle" (p. 64). And even

Madame notices Solange curtseying before her sister, Claire/"Madame" (p. 66).

The manipulation of personal pronouns is also important to the simultaneous maintenance of apparently opposed realms. At the beginning of the play, "Claire" addresses "Madame" in the third person: "Il m'est impossible d'oublier la poitrine de Madame sous le drapé de velours. Quand Madame soupire et parle à Monsieur de mon dévouement!" (p. 16). We cannot know whether she is speaking to the person before her, or referring to the absent Madame, or both at once. Ordinarily, when Madame addresses her servants she uses the familiar form <u>tu</u>; the maids respond with <u>vous</u>. Alone, Solange and Claire say <u>tu</u> to one another; in the presence of Madame they address each other with <u>vous</u>. During the ritual, the false Madame thus uses <u>tu</u> and the false maid <u>vous</u>. But even in their "profane" moments together, Claire will also at times say <u>vous</u> to Solange, seeming thereby to indicate sentiments or thoughts she in fact shares with the false Madame: "Dépêche-toi, nous n'avons pas le temps. Si la robe est trop longue, fais un ourlet avec des épingles de nourrice. . . . Tenez vos mains loin des miennes, votre contact est immonde. Dépêchez-vous" (p. 21). The two roles --"real" Claire and "false" Madame--apparently blend together at certain points. There is really nothing strange in this, for the maids, as we have seen, are always also in the presence of their image of Madame. "Madame" may also be speaking to both maids in the person of "Claire," <u>vous</u> being then the plural of <u>tu</u>. Later, however, when Solange says "nous sommes malheureuses," the spectator does not know whether she is speaking about herself and a supposedly absent Claire, or directly to Claire through the latter's disguise. The confusion of roles is, in short, quite profound; they cannot be said merely to alternate.

    Obviously, it is not by chance that the different levels of appearance interpenetrate this way; and such a compression of qualities is of course involved in any higher unification. The narrateur of <u>Le Journal du voleur</u> identifies the source of his trouble in that "en moi j'assume à la fois le rôle de victim et de criminel."[3] Earlier we saw that when Claire plays Madame, she becomes, in a similar fashion, both servant and mistress; when she appears to drink the poisoned tea, she is both sacrificer and sacrificed. Solange, on the other hand, while playing Claire, is both herself and her sister: hence, both martyr and criminal. Eventually donning Madame's white dress over her own black uniform, she is at once bride and mourner (or even deceased). Finally, even the names reinforce this evident tendency of conflicting elements to coexist within a single "entity." The seemingly indistinguishable maids are actually Claire and Sol-Ange (earth-angel), <u>lumière</u> and <u>ténèbres</u>: [Claire] J'y suis plus belle! Le danger m'auréole, Claire, et toi tu n'es que ténèbres . . . [Solange] . . . infernales! (p. 25).

The final scene of <u>Les Bonnes</u> presents us with an act of apparent "consecration," in which all the ritual elements apparently come together. Claire, playing Madame, though still dressed in maid's uniform, seems to drink the "poisoned" tea, while Solange, wearing Madame's white dress, stands immobile, her wrists crossed as if bound by handcuffs. In her soliloquy, she describes herself as also wearing "la toilette rouge des criminelles." Since the red dress is that usually worn by Claire/"Madame,"

Solange would then be all the characters at once (p. 87). Here the ritual seems to coalesce, attaining what critics have long considered a seemingly sought-after transcendent harmony, a oneness of mistress and maid, of Claire and Solange, of criminal and saint, of sacrificer and scapegoat.

> Tu seras seule pour assumer nos deux existences. Il te faudra beaucoup de force. Personne ne saura au bagne que je t'accompagne en cachette. Et surtout, quand tu seras condamnée, n'oublie pas que tu me portes en toi. Précieusement (pp. 91-2).

This supposed transubstantiation of "opposites" would, according to Coe, permit the maids to free themselves from their ugly world, while yet remaining in it, to destroy and yet simultaneously to liberate themselves along the traditional lines established by the Christian martyrs.[5] This final moment and apparent farewell would then also be a re-enactment of <u>la scène/Cène</u> to which Genet referred in his "Lettre à

Pauvert," the cup of tea replacing the chalice of wine. The result of this "Aufhebung" would be a marvelous new substance held up or "elevated" for adoration before the audience in a final ritual gesture: "Maintenant nous sommes Mademoiselle Solange Lemercier. La femme Lemercier. La Lemercier. La fameuse criminelle" (p. 90).[6]

In the sacrament of the Mass, Christian ritual is an evocation of the Real Presence, the full presence of the Divine under the appearance of bread and wine, with whom the communicant unites himself. What then would be the transcendent <u>telos</u> of Genet's ritual? The narrator of <u>Le Journal du voleur</u> once again provides a suggestion.

> Je n'osais regarder ses bras.
> Ils étaient si fort Armand que
> je craignais de m'être jusqu'
> alors trompé en m'adressant à
> ses yeux ou à sa bouche. Ceux-
> ci, ou ce qu'ils exprimaient
> n'avaient d'autre réalité que
> celle qui soudain venait à se
> créer par l'entrelacs de ses

> bras devant un torse de lutteur.
> Qu'ils se dénouent, la plus aiguë, la plus exacte réalité d'Armand sera dissoute.
>
> Or j'apprends aujourd'hui que ce noeud de muscles j'eusse rougi de le regarder parce qu'ils me découvrait Armand. Si l'étendard du roi porté par un chevalier au galop apparaît seul, nous pouvons être ému, nous découvrir, si le roi l'apportait lui-même nous serions terrassé. Le raccourci que propose le symbole porté par ce qu'il doit signifier donne et détruit la signification et la chose signifiée. (Et tout s'aggravait de ce que la torsade couvrait le torse!)[7]

Most critics have argued that, by means of what this essay has called a ritual "transubstantiation," Genet's characters are in fact only coming to participate in the "impossible nullité" to which we also find allusion in <u>Le Journal du voleur</u>. They would thus elevate and complete themselves in a self-comprehending **void**; they would attain what Lewis T. Cetta identifies as a "negative apotheosis."[8]

But does Genet's "Christian ritual" really seem to seek such a transcendent union, whether positive or negative, full presence or full absence? Earlier this essay attempted to show that Les Bonnes exaggerates and thereby highlights problems with the system of cyclical mimetic ritual, at the same time raising the question of the very relation between presence and absence. We should now ask whether Genet does not also modify the Christian ritual of transcendence, undermining in yet other ways than those discussed earlier, the all-important notions of identity and difference on which it is based, and thereby thwarting in advance any desire to see his characters as striving for ultimate peace and reconciliation in a final sublime moment.

There is, in the first place, never any radical or "pure" difference in Les Bonnes. From either a synchronic or diachronic perspective, sacred ritual and profane reality, as we have seen, both interrupt and flow into one another. The same can be said about illusion and reality in Genet's theater as a whole. The realist stage setting ("la copie à peu près exacte d'une chambre féminine") ironically prescribed by the playwright is actually no less theatrical than "les robes monstrueuses" worn by the maids or the painted screens of <u>Les Paravents</u>.[9] Similarly, and as this essay has suggested, maids and mistress are not so completely differentiated as one might first expect. Genet even underlines their resemblance by playing on the double meaning of <u>bonne</u>. If Claire and Solange are <u>bonnes</u>, Madame is also <u>bonne</u> (p. 38). And, of course, the social statuses of both servant and master are always mutually implicated.

>C'est grâce à moi que tu es,
et tu me nargues! Tu ne peux
savoir comment il est pénible
d'être Madame, Claire, d'être
le prétexte à vos simagrées!
Il me suffirait de si peu et
tu n'existerais plus (p. 23).

Here, "Madame" seems to overlook the fact that, although without the master there can never be a servant, the reverse is also true. In addition, we have seen that, since the maids' profanatory ritual is organized around both a certain vision of "Madame"/Madame as sacrificial victim and apparent fact of the maids' repeated self-debasement, each becomes a scapegoat for the other. More obviously, there is little to distinguish the maids themselves--so little, in fact, that Madame appears to confuse them: "Madame a soigné Claire ou Solange, car Madame nous confondait toujours" (p. 72). Claire ("light") and Sol-Ange ("earth-angel") are also, it should here be noted, Claire and Sol-Ange ("sun-angel"). The names of the two sisters, then, evoke that of Lucifer, the radiant fallen angel, who is no doubt the most ambiguous figure in the Judeo-Christian tradition. Like him, the maids are both saintly and criminal--holy in their isolation from the world, evil in their daring transgressions. Even the difference between the sexes--the male/female dichotomy--may be in question here. The characters do not appear simply sexually inverted, rather they seem marked by sexual uncertainty. The description provided in "Comment jouer Les Bonnes"(itself a highly ambivalent text, as the jouer of the title suggests) contains, for example, both female and male elements. Each member of the biological "opposition" is already implied in the other. This questioning of pure difference is, we must recall, the cause of that joy the narrator describes in Le Journal du voleur after he steals a policeman's cape.[10]

Just as we find no pure difference, however, we also find--despite what several critics have asserted--no simple identity in the works of Genet.[11] The notion itself relies, at least implicitly, on either religious faith or belief in the efficacy of mimetic magic. But, for Genet, the characters are always only *approximate* mirror images: "Vous êtes nos miroirs *déformants*" (p. 83--emphasis added); "Jamais nous ne pourrons remplacer Madame" (p. 63). In the description of Armand cited above from Le Journal du voleur, the signifier must completely cover the signified for there to be an Aufhebung; the torsade must coincide with the torse, Armand's arms with his essence, the king's banner with the king's authority. Yet if this were ever the case in Les Bonnes, the ritual "murder" of the false Madame would be identical with the real murder of Madame, the false Madame

with the real <u>patronne</u>, the false Claire with
the real Claire, and, by extension, Claire with
Madame and Solange with Claire. Such "identi-
ties" are always undercut, however, for the
various elements can never be fully subsumed into one another. Something is always missing or
left over, just as for this to occur something
has to be left out, here the "ad." Thus, the
ritual murder is never the real murder, the
false Madame is never the real <u>patronne</u>, etc.
Neither can it be said that any substantial
transformation or transubstantiation occurs.
There may be compression, interinvolvement, or
superimposition of images, words, and characters
in <u>Les Bonnes</u>, but not a radical unitary change
of their whole substance, as in the Eucharistic
liturgy. The character described by Solange in
her soliloquy, and presumably created in the
final scene, "La Le-mercier," for example, would
be the couple Solange-Claire simultaneously ne-
gated and preserved in the elevation to a higher level. But the play never actually shows us
such <u>Aufhebung</u>. The curtain falls before the
necessary corpse. There is, in other words, no
"transcendent" union in <u>Les Bonnes</u>, no perfect
merger, only a continual shifting and overlap-

ping, a dynamic form of coexistence or interplay among elements.

This discussion does not intend to imply, however, (as does Coe) that Genet's play is actually striving for a negative form of <u>Aughebung</u> but, unfortunately, fails. Neither does it agree with Sartre's assertion that what replaces the desire for transcendence is a series of sterile <u>tourniquets</u>.[12] Such interpretations destroy "le bonheur de l'équivoque" be restricting the playful ambivalence of supposed "opposites." The trouble that the narrator of <u>Le Journal du voleur</u> experiences, for example, when he assumes simultaneously the roles of victim and criminal, or of criminal and policeman, is, in fact, a confusion, agitation, and even sexual excitement created by that very form of ambiguity inherent in his situation.[13]

NOTES

[1] In <u>Des choses cachées depuis la fondation du monde</u>, Girard rejects the usual, and institutionalized, interpretation of Christ's death on the cross as an expiatory sacrifice (pp. 204-5). Of course Girard's own revision-

ist interpretation must then also diverge sharply from previous thinking on the scene of the Last Supper, as described in the synoptic gospels. This in turn will involve him, openly or tacitly, in a repudiation of certain basic elements of the Catholic Mass, notably the sacrament of the Eucharist, as well as of the analogous portions of any Protestant service (e.g., Calvinist or Lutheran) in which the Crucifixion of the Son is explicitly designated a sacrifice. In fact, Girard seems rather to avoid the question altogether by discretely privileging the Gospel of St. John which includes no mention of the Last Supper. Other religious writers will generally insist that Christian ceremonies are not entirely free from the traces of the older sacrificial rite, while certain pagan mystery cults were already in some ways transcendental. "The proclamation of the death and resurrection of Jesus Christ," as Wilhelm Heitmüller has pointed out in "Hellenistic Christianity Before Paul," trans. W. Meeks, <u>The Writings of St. Paul</u>, ed. W. Meeks (New York: W. W. Norton and Co., 1972), ". . . must immediately enter in pagan minds into an amalgamation with similar stories of the violent death

and exaltation of gods" (p. 317). The events
of Holy Week, read during the Mass as the Passion of Christ, certainly recall the scenario
of the periodic festivals: the triumphant entry into Jerusalem on Palm Sunday; the betrayal
and trial; the scourging and crowning with thorns;
the execution of the "mock" king on Calvary.
This degradation is followed by the glorious resurection on Easter Sunday. Similarly, the Mass
itself is seen by the Catholic Church as "l'offrande renouvelée du même sacrifice une fois offerte sur la croix"--see, <u>Dictionnaire de théologie catholique</u>, Tome 10, Partie I (Paris: Librairie Létouzey et Ané, 1928), p. 1287. Nor
has the primitive conception of periodic regeneration of the world through annual repetition of
the Creation been eliminated, but rather only
translated into Christian terms. Although the
events of Christ's life are said to have taken
place in historic time, they are also considered
to have occurred "in the beginning," since, suggests Eliade, "pour le Chrétien le Temps commence
de nouveau avec la naissance du Christ, car l'incarnation fonde une nouvelle situation de l'homme
dans le Cosmos"--<u>L'Eternel retour</u>, pp. 193-4; see
also, <u>Le sacré et le profane</u> (Paris: Gallimard,

1965), p. 97. The liturgical cycle that annually repeats the events of Christ's life may be seen, then, as a substitute for the pagan cycle of death and renewal. (Again Girard presents a somewhat discordant view when he asserts that with Christ, "l'histoire cyclique est terminée du fait même que son ressort commence à apparaître"--Choses cachées, p. 229.) Among those pagan mystery cults containing elements of transcendentalism, on the other hand, were, for example, the cults of Attis, Osiris, and Mithras. By means of initiation, adherents were thought to attain union with the divinity and thus to partake in the immortality for which they yearned. Through these sacraments, they ceased to be natural men, and were reborn into a higher state of being--see, Albert Schweitzer, "Eschatological Mystic," p. 387, and Martin Dibelius, "Mystic and Prophet," p. 396, in The Writings of St. Paul.

[2] Canons 1-2, Council of Trent, discussed in Dictionnaire de théologie catholique, Tome 5, Partie II, pp. 1343-50. Genet, "Lettre à Pauvert," p. 146.

[3] Genet, Journal, p. 16.

[4] See, e.g., Lewis T. Cetta, Profane Play,

Ritual, and Jean Genet: A Study of His Drama
(University, Alabama: University of Alabama
Press, 1974), p. 44; Coe, pp. 43, 141; or Zimbardo, pp. 252-3. Cetta finds a similar merger
of life and death in the apotheosis of the Chief
of Police at the end of *Le Balcon*. His mausoleum is "the huge, fertile, life-giving symbol of
the phallus united forever with the sterile,
dead rock" (p. 53). Sartre's formulation is
more problematic: "Il vivra le déchirement *comme*
unité; sa volonté posera l'incompatibilité des
deux thèses et décidera souverainement de leur
unité foncière" (p. 308).

[5] Coe, pp. 158-9; 198; see also Zimbardo,
p. 253.

[6] It would be shown that a similar "transfiguration" occurs in *Notre Dame des Fleurs*:
"Dans sa robe de faille bleu pâle, bordée de valencienne blanche, il était plus que lui-même.
Il était lui-même et son complément. . . .
Notre Dame levait son bras nu et--c'est merveilleux--cet assassin avait tout juste le geste
à peine plus brutal qu'aurait eu certainement,
pour chiffonner son chignon, Emilienne d'Alençon"
(p. 119). Sartre, in his discussion of this passage, describes Notre Dame as "supérieur à la

fois aux jeunes hommes et à toutes les femmes."
"Cet être hybride, et l'espèce des centaures
et des sirènes, commence en mâle et s'achève
dans le néant, en feu d'artifice femelle"
(<u>Saint Genet</u>, p. 563).

    7 Genet, <u>Journal</u>, p. 215.

    8 Genet, <u>Journal</u>, p. 100: "Le livre, <u>Journal du voleur</u>: poursuite de l'Impossible Nullité"; Cetta, p. 20. See also Sartre, pp. 310-11 (in which it is suggested that "Genet atteindra dans l'anéantissement absolu la plénitude d'être"); and Brustein, p. 384. It may perhaps seem unwarranted to call this search for "full absence" a modified version of the Christian ritual, rather than considering it, with Cetta, an example of an Oriental striving --Hindu or Taoist--that regards as the Highest and Absolute, as God, pure nothingness. This eastern world-view would seem all the more appropriate because of its belief in natural avatars and metempsychosis. Yet, it appears inappropriate to call the "teleological" aspect of <u>Les Bonnes</u> "eastern," since it retains a necessary material component that is apparently transcended while nevertheless remaining in appearance preserved (i.e., <u>aufgehoben</u>). Sartre

seems to suggest this latter view in his discussion of gesture in <u>Saint Genet</u> (pp. 292-3). In the oriental religions, as Hegel explains, "the annihilating of spiritual and physical existence has nothing concrete in it; and absorption in the abstractly Universal has no connection with the real" (<u>Philosophy of History</u>, p. 158). Genet's ritual requires some concrete element, even if it is only a theatrical property.

⁹ Genet, "Comment jouer <u>Les Bonnes</u>," p. 12.

¹⁰ Genet, <u>Journal</u>, p. 34.

¹¹ See, e.g., Zimbardo, pp. 252-3 and Coe, pp. 141, 146.

¹² Coe, pp. 187, 269; Sartre, pp. 305-14.

¹³ Genet hints at this love of interplay in "Comment jouer <u>Les Bonnes</u>" (p. 21), and makes it still clearer in the stage directions for <u>Les Paravents</u>: "Se confrontant aux objets dessinés en trompe-l'oeil sur chaque paravent, il devra toujours y avoir sur la scène un ou plusieurs objets réels . . . destiné[s] à confronter leur propre réalité avec les objets dessinés" (Décines: L'Arbalète, 1961-1976), pp. 9-10.

IV   CREATIVE POSSIBILITIES

In conclusion, it would seem possible to say that <u>Les Bonnes</u>, while retaining in some ways the basic patterns of both primitive and Christian ritual, nonetheless renders those patterns highly problematic as well. Instead of the reassuring familiarity of either simple repetition or transcendent totalization, we find a "playful" equivocation that implies a "serious" questioning of both mimetic cyclicality and a more conventional ontological escatology.[1] The maintenance of ambiguity or ambivalence might lend to Genet's theater a more decidedly "irritating" view of the world process than many critics have usually allowed it.

As this essay sought to demonstrate, the large-scale cultural hypotheses of René Girard, for one, sees in this failure or refusal to draw clear-cut distinctions or present discrete options a particularly dangerous threat to the entire structure of civilization. The attitude of <u>Violence and the Sacred</u> toward such "playful" equivocation or what this paper will call "agonistic play" becomes apparent in its discussion of the ancient <u>agon</u>. The prize of that struggle--for it must end with one adversary being declared victorious--is divinity itself in the form of glorious violence or <u>kudos</u>, the "talisman of supremacy." For Girard, therefore, all contests and competitions--in this he includes every form of play, e.g., games of skill and chance, athletic matches and even sexual activity--are engaged in for the sake of total mastery; the adversary must be vanquished. Because the actual object awarded at the conclusion of these activities is ephemeral and may consequently appear worthless, "we tend to assume," Girard continues, "that the contest itself, no matter how perilous, is only a pastime, an event of limited interest to the protagonists, mere 'sport.'" This is not the case, however, nor is it "some vulgar trophy or second-rate divinity the adversaries are trying to wrest from each other's grasp, but their very souls, their vital force, their being."[2] Being, then, as we saw earlier, is the ultimate prize and it is here related to mastery. Only as supreme can one really be. Only as a self-identical, self-totalized entity can one have true being. Only then can one be truly divine. Once again we find ourselves in the realm of traditional

metaphysics. Moreover, it appears that the
Girardian hypothesis cannot conceive of any
agonistic play in which the attainment of mastery, while it might remain an impetus to striving, might not be the sole purpose and <u>telos</u> of
the contest. It cannot deal adequately, in other words, with any playful strife, like, that
of <u>Les Bonnes</u>, in which the excitement and stimulation of the struggle appears more important
than the pleasure of consummated victory.

    Playful strife, however, need not be
limited to the most obvious forms of <u>agon</u>. It
is inherent, for example, in all works of art
and particularly in theatrical representation.
Similarly, it is to be found in those structures
and institutions that allow for questioning and
contestation. Yet, even these forms of play appear monstrous in <u>Violence and the Sacred</u>, for
they are always related in some way or other to
the violent conflicts of non-differentiation
and therefore ultimately to cultural chaos. The
con-test or strife that ambiguity and any other
active interplay of elements or forces necessarily involves are, in other words, understood as,
essentially and therefore inevitably, an impetus to destruction. Its constructive side, we

recall, is for the most part considered a mere retrospective projection, made only once the scapegoat mechanism has succeeded in bringing generalized violence under control. Alternatively, conflict may appear to have an inherently positive dimension, when it is organized within, or as, that very (and consequently very ambiguous) mechanism itself. According to the Girardian hypothesis, however, playful strife or agonistic play cannot in itself--i.e., outside the institution of the scapegoating process and the cultural unanimity it fosters--have any saving function. Indeed, even in or as this one exceptional form, it is still linked directly to violence and hence to the possibility of cultural destabilization. For Girard this always means the danger, or even the likelihood of pure destructiveness (i.e., nihilism). Even in its most life-enhancing form(s), therefore, the *agon* is ultimately to be transcended.

There are other critics, of course, who demonstrate some awareness of the creative possibilities inherent in the ritual play of Genet's theater. Their conception of the latter is generally somewhat limited however. In one group are those who, like Martin Esslin following Sartre, perceive such play a purely solipsistic form of escapism, an individual's flight from "the hall of mirrors of the human condition." The critics here would seem to have in mind primarily that variety of pretense, or role-taking, that allows for a playing-out in artistic or poetic fantasy of personal obsessions that could not otherwise be mastered. This theory of "psycho-drama" assigns to the playful conflict of the <u>agon</u> merely its traditional cathartic function.[3] As such it is ultimately conservative, limiting--if not eliminating--the (imaginative) play's capacity for a genuinely creative effect on the structure or tenor of society.

A second group of more socially oriented critics and historians has, by contrast, seen in all "genuinely" agonistic play and every play-ful conflict, the possibility of a rehearsal for political transformation. In the freer atmosphere of "sacred," or carnival time, for example, radical alternatives, otherwise regarded as simply fantastic and even monstrous--i.e., outside the established limits of feasible good order, hence, excessive in every sense--including the possibility of a very different perhaps less generally oppressive, distribution of social power and authority, may now be given "serious" consideration and even acted out. The carnival spirit, as discussed by Bakhtin, Davis, and others, is or involves, on the most visceral level, the appeal to a different order whose flexibility and openness would perhaps make it at once more life-enhancing and better able to manage social conflict and tensions without either repression or collapse. When, moreover, the time and circumstances are suitable, their playful, yet generally contestatory, spirit might well begin, imperceptibly, to melt into definite revolutionary action. In his analysis of Les Nègres, for example, Goldmann has suggested that the "destruction of the caricatural Whites will oblige the Blacks to discover authentic words of love, original gestures, a truly Black culture rooted in their own essence, which they have discovered"--and "discovered" through their own forms of ritual play.[4]

These socio-political dimensions of contestatory play do not, however, exhaust its creative potential, nor, by extension, that of Genet's theater. For insofar as it proves capable of a quasi-mimetic testing and even challenging of a broad range of conventional attitudes and concepts (e.g., the absolutism implied and at times proclaimed, by our traditional logic of identity and difference), that theater may in fact be clearing space for fresh approaches to problems in every domain. Beyond this "merely" critical function, it may be said thereby to provide, or itself to become, precisely the sort of Spiel-raum required by all movements, change or differentiation. This crucial leeway--an essential factor in all such more or less creative endeavors as, for example, social criticism, literary interpretation, scientific revolution or artistic innovation--will, of course, somewhat unhinge institutionalized patterns of thought and behavior and necessarily so. Yet this alone cannot be ground for considering it simply destructive. For, even at its most radical the truly playful criticism never simply destroys. At the very least it continues to require the tradition with which it plays. And while the space it clears, or is, may certainly make or allow some significant difference in established structures it may also and at the same time revitalize those institutions by restoring their ability to accommodate challenge and change. Thus, even Girard is willing to admit that a completely static structure--such as his scapegoat theory of culture ultimately seems to be recommending with its either/or choice between mass unanimity and chaotic barbarism--such narrowness and rigidity cannot allow for the sort of thinking that leads to discovery.[5] With regard to the latter, moreover, we may ask, finally, quite seriously, whether Genet's dramatic re-vision of problems like those of identity and difference or representation are really very much less perceptive that those of Nietzsche, Heidegger, or Derrida. It appears, then, that there must also be a certain tense interplay between the desire to do "violence" to existing structures and the recognition of a need to maintain them, for there to be anything like genuine intellectual activity in the work. And some room for play, indeed, for a degree of what this essay has called playful strife or conflict, may be necessary for there to be any truly creative inter-course in any sense at all.[6]

In its own discussion of the relationship between Les Bonnes and the two most prevalent and powerful model structures of ritual practice, moreover, this essay has been obliged to invoke the still more challenging notion of creative repetition.[7] The latter may in this case be understood as a re-playing that reinterprets traditional patterns by continually reinscribing them in modified and varied forms. It does not mean a second coming of the exactly identical thing. Rather it suggests that tradition offers a range of heretofore undeveloped resources that may still be realizable. We may respond to them, however, in many ways. We may select some and reject others, challenge those that have been dominant and attempt to recover those that have been suppressed, or yet bring forward those problematic (and for that reason often obscured) ones so that they may be critically examined. We have demonstrated, for example, how the maids' ritual exploits certain ambiguities already inherent in the primitive periodic rites, e.g., the "dual natures" of both violence and the sacred, or the ambivalent status of the scapegoat. At the same time we saw how the play, by the way it differs from the archaic rite that it nonetheless in some ways repeats, calls into question the concept of being or presence on which its cyclical mimeticism appears to be founded. There is, in other words, no pure continuity. Neither, however, is there any pure discontinuity, although some degree of change appears inevitable. New events, including new possibilities will always arise, albeit (necessarily) conditioned by the past. Repetition, then, involves the "handing down" to ourselves of possibilities, "but not necessarily <u>as</u> having thus come down."[8] It may be seen as a return of a certain inventive force. In Genet's theater, it suggests non-traditional modes of perceiving, e.g., the relationship between one character and another, between the stage and the audience[9] (or the text and the reader), between the text and its political and social context, perhaps even between art and life. Consequently, the potentiality of such creative repetition may be said to cast doubt on the traditional interpretations of Genet's theater as amounting to nothing more than a series of sterile, narcissistic whirligigs.

When we turned to a discussion of the relationship between <u>Les Bonnes</u> and the Catholic Mass, we attempted to show how this re-petitioning of tradition might in yet other ways stimulate contestation of the concept of presence and the related search for (transcendent) oneness. To emphasize play in this context is to suggest, as have recent Continental philosophers and critics, that, being as identity or full presence, which Girard has called the goal of (ritual) mimesis, and which is the putative center of the Eucharistic sacrament, should be regarded, in Derrida's words, "comme présence ou absence à partir de la possibilité du jeu et non l'inverse." Le jeu, in other words, is here understood as "la disruption de la présence," because it sees the presence of an element always only as "une référence significante et substitutive inscrite dans un système de différence et le mouvement d'une chaîne."[10] If totalization is impossible, it is because the field of possible substitutions excludes totalization. And this, not because it is infinite or inexhaustible, but because it lacks a stable center, origin or telos, that could check the freedom of substitution. Radically conceived, as this paper has argued it is in Les Bonnes, play is consequently something exceeding Girard's mere alternation of presence and absence, identity and difference. Instead, within its artistic design is fixed the interinvolvement of such

supposed opposites. The work maintains them
apart while nevertheless holding them together,
so that the gap experienced in that interplay
is "itself" always enabled visibly to persist
in its <u>ek-sistence</u>, or its being what which it
is.[11] In Genet's theater, that is, such <u>Risse</u>
become perceptible, for example, when the superimposed layers do not exactly cover each other,
when, to return to the playwright's phrase, the
<u>torsade</u> does not entirely hide the <u>torse</u>. This
arrangement of forces "in play" produces a contest enjoyed for its own sake. What is important in the ritual of <u>Les Bonnes</u>, in other words,
may not be the consummation of an act, but, rather, as we observed above, the exciting and here
even dangerous foreplay. Mastery is no longer
the sole possible issue. The players in this
<u>agon</u>--whether Claire and Solange, the maids and
Madame, the sacred and the profane, or archaic
ritual and Catholic Mass--are encouraged to
close in such a way that they at once conceal
and unconceal each other. Through comparison
they reveal each other to the extent that they
are different. Yet, at the same time, that difference can never be completely reduced to the
knowable. Something is always denied or refused

if only because, in bringing one aspect into focus others must necessarily be for that moment relatively less important, muted, or even obscured. Even the sameness that seems to have been revealed will often in fact conceal the remaining degree of the adversary's irreducible alterity. This concealing/unconcealing, the creative strife, may be said to occur in innovative works of art like the play we have been considering.

The possibilities of creative repetition and contestatory play may, finally, be related to that elevation through the theater suggested in Genet's "Lettre à Pauvert." The "elevating" role of Genet's art, it might be argued, is to intensify awareness of, and further release from, the vicious cycles and thwarted attempts at <u>Aufhebung</u> it critically repeats, and to intimate indirectly the possibility of more creative relationships, in art and life, that it perhaps cannot directly represent. The play of <u>Les Bonnes</u>, ritual and otherwise, might, in other words, point to a creative force that, because it is not a "presence" but rather a network of dynamic relationships cannot actually be reproduced. This interplay can be staged (<u>mis</u>

en scène), but never re-presented (mis en Cène). It is inénarrable (cf. p. 52). Moreover, these relationships, as we have seen, do not simply "transcend" all forms of contestation including self-contestation. On the contrary, they require such continued testing and striving. Provocative play-fulness might then be considered fundamental to Genet's art, an art that takes shape less as a narrative of human appropriation and domination, than as the drama of man's participation in a world he can never entirely master.[12]

NOTES

[1] In the 1954 version of Les Bonnes, this ambivalence was clearly reduced by modifying the use of personal pronouns as well as the extent of the intrusion of ritual into "reality" and "reality" into ritual (e.g., pp. 19, 28, 64; 17, 85; 63, 66). More significant, however, were the changes made in the final run-through of the ritual and particularly in the last scene. In this later version, Claire, rather than Solange, wears Madame's white dress over her black uniform, and the play no longer ends with a "con-

secration." Instead, Solange proudly announces the liberation of the maids. The reduction of dramatic tension here is no doubt one important reason why the revision is generally felt to result in an inferior theatrical production.

 2 Girard, Violence, pp. 152-4.

 3 Martin Esslin, The Theater of the Absurd, revised edition (Garden City, N.Y.: Doubleday and Co., Anchor Books, 1969), pp. 166-97; Sartre, p. 501ff. The understanding of the problem appears to reproduce on the level of the individual psyche that certain, limited, and still rather dangerous form of imagination freedom Girard is willing to allow--indeed, cautiously to insist upon--on the level of the community (Violence, p. 99).

 4 For concrete and detailed examples and discussions of the no doubt subtle and ambiguous, yet nonetheless real insurrectionary aspects or tendencies of the carnival, see the recent work of Emmanuel LeRoy Ladurie, Carnival in Romans, trans. M. Feeney (New York: George Braziller, 1979), as well as Davis, "The Reasons of Misrule," pp. 97-123. Goldmann, "The Theater of Genet," p. 231.

 5 Girard, Violence, p. 237.

[6] See, e.g., Martin Heidegger, "The Origin of the Work of Art," trans. A. Hofstadter, in *Poetry, Language, Thought* (1971; rpt. New York: Harper and Row, Harper Colophon Books, 1975), pp. 15-88.

[7] This notion of creative repetition has been developed extensively in the works of Heidegger and Derrida, and has now begun to be employed in a somewhat more strictly empirical fashion in this country (see, e.g., LaCapra's *Preface to Sartre*).

[8] Martin Heidegger, *Being and Time*, p. 435. See also Jacques Derrida, "Cartouches," *La Vérité en peinture* (Paris: Flammarion, 1978).

[9] The question of the relationship between the play and the audience in *Les Bonnes* has been actively debated. Genet's theater cannot, of course, depend like either primitive or Christian ritual, on a relation of religious faith. And yet it has seemed to many critics that Genet tries to substitute instead something that will make the spectator at least wish to believe. The extreme emotion and involvement of the religious experience may, they argue, be reproduced by other equally powerful stimuli. In support of this argument Coe identifies three

such stimuli, most effective when all present simultaneously: sex, racial antagonism, and politics (pp. 258-60; also Cetta, p. 9). But is anything like such a religious experience ever really created here? Is the audience not perhaps put at a distance, in fact excluded from the stage? Some may even see it as present only to be shocked, alienated, insulted like Madame. Genet has written that in viewing a performance of <u>Les Bonnes</u>, the spectator is to be made to feel uneasy. Rather than "communication ou rien," as Bataille suggests (p. 206), we find a malaise created by ambiguity or ambivalence, neither belief nor disbelief, but both at once. As Genet has himself, and somewhat paradoxically explained in "Comment jouer <u>Les Bonnes</u>": "Il faut à la fois y croire et refuser d'y croire" (p. 10).

[10] Jacques Derrida, "La Structure, le signe et le jeu dans le discours des sciences humaines," <u>L'Ecriture et la différence</u> (Paris: Seuil, 1967(, pp. 426-7.

[11] Heidegger, "Origin of the Work of Art," pp. 49, 53-5, 39.

[12] This view of the possibly positive relation between ambiguity and playfulness, on

the one hand, and creativity, intellectual or artistic, on the other, has been explored extensively, though in a somewhat different context, by LaCapra in his <u>Preface</u> <u>to</u> <u>Sartre</u>.

DEGRÉ SECOND

BISHOP, MICHAEL: The Language of Poetry Crisis and Solution. Studies in Modern Poetry of French Expression, 1945 of the present. (Degré Second 1). Amsterdam 1980. 276 pp. Hfl. 60,–

Contents: Acknowledgements; Introduction - Michael Bishop; The Language of René Char - James Lawler; Henri Michaux: Impetus and Infinity - Peter Broome; Francis Ponge - Ian Higgins; Evoking the 'objet profound': The Poetry of Yves Bonnefoy - Graham Dunstan Martin; Jacques Dupin - Brian Gill; Musing: Michel Duguy's Language as Mask and Matrix - Mary Ann Caws; Denis Roche - Michael Bishop; Aimé Césaire: Miraculous Weapons, Enduring Shackles - A. James Arnold; 'Je danse, donc je suis': The Rhythm of Léopold Sédar Senghor's Two Cultures - Roger Little; Tchicaya U Tam'si - Gerald Moore; The Power of the Word in Marie-Claire d'Orbaix's 'Erosion du silence' - James W. Brown; Gaston Miron - John Beaver; Bio-Bibliographical Notes on Poets; Notes on Contributors; Index.

BUSBY, KEITH: Gauvain in Old French Literature. Amsterdam 1980. (Degré Second 2). 425 pp. Hfl. 85,–

This study analyses the rôle of the figure of Gauvain, the nephew of King Arthur, in French literature during the period 1155-1225. An Introduction reviews previous scholarship in the field and defines the aims and methods of the study. Subsequent chapters are devoted to: texts before Chrétien de Troyes; the Early Romances of Chrétien; Chréstien's 'Le Conte du Graal'; the Later Grail Romances; non-Grail Romances after Chrétien de Troyes; the Vulgate Cycle. A Conclusion draws together evidence from the previous chapters and shows that a gradual but definite change can be discerned in the way in which authors treat the figure. The liberty with which authors depict Gauvain for their own purposes can be said to result from the fact that his accumulated characteristics do not render him suitable for use as a hero. As well students of French literature, this book will also be of interest to Anglicists and Germanists. The author teaches in the Departments of English and Comparative Literature in the University of Utrecht.

TIEFENBRUN, SUSAN W.: Signs of the Hidden. Semiotic Studies. Amsterdam 1980. 237 pp. (Degré Second 3) Hfl. 50,–

This study involves the construction and application of an esthetic metalanguage designed to penetrate the surface of a highly specialized and eminently analyzable discourse known as literature. The esthetic metalanguage which constructed and applied to various genres within literary texts of seventeenth-century France is rooted in semiotics, in that elusive and fleeting relationship between form and content, signifier and signified, the rarefield place of the hidden. Semiotics is the science of signs. The science was born at about the turn of the twentieth century, when two scholars in different but related fields of linguistics and philosophy were investigating the elements of signifying systems.

KARS, H.: Le portrait chez Marivaux: études d'un type de segment textuel. Aspects Métadiscursifs, Définitionnels, Formels. Amsterdam 1981. 252 pp. (Degré Second 4). Hfl. 50,–

Qu'est-ce qu'un "portrait" en littérature? H. Kars a entrepris d'examiner ce phénomène — si familier, si fondamental et pourtant si mal défini — dans l'oeuvre d'un écrivain qui, parmi les portraitistes du XVIIIe siècle, n'est certainement pas le moins remarquable. L'auteur étudie la manière dont Marivaux parle lui-même du portrait, et pose la question de savoir dans quelle mesure ce "métadiscours" peut révéler une "poétique" du portrait. Il examine la tradition du concept de "portrait", et s'attache à chercher des critères pour une définition nouvelle, applicable au corpus exploré. Une dernière partie de l'ouvrage est consacrée à l'analyse des particularités formelles que présente le portrait sur les plans syntaxique, stylistique et rhétorique.

USA/Canada	: Humanities Press Inc., 171 First Avenue, ATLANTIC HIGHLANDS, N.J. 07716
Japan	: United Publishers Services, Shimura Building, 1-4, chome, Kojimachi, Chiyoda-ku, TOKYO
And others	: Editions Rodopi N.V., Keizersgracht 302-304, 1016 EX AMSTERDAM, Telephone (020) – 22 75 07